Managing Your Search Project

Plan your search.
Measure progress.
Get results.

LEE HECHT
HARRISON

More options. Better results.

Version 2.0

Lee Hecht Harrison supports recycling and other efforts to preserve our environment for our future workforce leaders and the world.

What's Inside

Your Road Map to Success

What is the Blended Learning Version?

Career transition learning content and methods have changed along with technology. The goal of the Managing Your Search Project/Blended Learning Version is to lead the engaged candidate through the 10 Milestones of MYSP, yet also offer a guide to other learning alternatives and expanded samples on LHH's premier website: the Career Resource Network (CRN). Candidates are encouraged to utilize the increasingly sophisticated e-learning programs and podcasts.

The Career Resource Network's website address is Career.lhh.com. You'll want to bookmark it now. You'll find yourself referring to it often during the course of your job search project – and long after.

Once you register for the CRN, you are a member for life. Even after your program ends, you will have alumni privileges, including access to the CRN alumni website.

Getting Started

For many, beginning a job search may seem like a daunting task. Beyond the emotional impact, you may have questions such as: What do I want to do? What do I need to do? Where do I start?

These materials will help you find answers to these questions. In addition to the information and techniques, you will learn career management skills you can use throughout your career.

This program reflects more than 40 years of experience that Lee Hecht Harrison has had in career transition and career management. As the premier career management firm, we have pioneered new methods of career transition and career management using advanced technology, the Internet, performance benchmarks and teams.

The Managing Your Search Project/Blended Learning Version takes you through each phase of the AIM process: Assess Opportunity, Implement Search and Manage Transition. It provides a logical order to this vitally important project you have taken on – job search.

This book also provides worksheets, checklists and assessments that will help you do the following and much more:

- Discover your true value
- Complete your winning resume
- Develop your online brand
- Create your marketing plan
- Realize the value of your network
- Utilize social media
- Choose your next employer
- Negotiate your salary

Your Lee Hecht Harrison program gives you an opportunity to learn from our experience helping hundreds of thousands of candidates through career transition.

You may be eager to get started, but it is well worth taking the time to read the entire program introduction.

It will provide you with an overview of the entire project that you're about to undertake. The introduction also will provide you with valuable information on how to maintain the high level of productivity so necessary for a successful search.

We understand career transition is an emotional roller coaster. This book will help jump-start your efforts and lead you towards a proactive approach.

The AIM Process

AIM is Lee Hecht Harrison's proprietary three-stage business approach to career transition. The three phases of AIM are divided into 10 milestones to guide you through your search, as illustrated below:

 A **I** **M**

ASSESS OPPORTUNITY

IMPLEMENT SEARCH

MANAGE TRANSITION

1. Survey Your Professional Environment

2. Determine Your Professional Objective

3. Create Your Communications Strategy

4. Define Your Target Market

5. Gather Marketplace Information

6. Get Your Message Out

7. Talk with Hiring Managers

8. Consider Other Methods of Search

9. Interview, Cultivate Offers and Negotiate

10. Transition into a New Position

Career Transition Is an Opportunity to Improve Your Career

In the day-to-day crunch of work and deadlines, most people do not have the time, energy or expertise to manage their careers as effectively as they could.

A career transition made while unemployed can have some significant negatives, including stress, uncertainty and concern about lost income. However, it can be seen as presenting a number of opportunities for those who know how to take advantage of them.

The possibilities include:

- **Achieving a higher level of satisfaction with your work.** Knowing what is important to you and what you really want to do next in your career allows you to identify and pursue jobs and organizations where your contributions are valued and rewarded and your skills fully used.

- **Joining a new organization with values compatible with your own.** As part of this transition, you will be given the chance to assess the things that are really important to you personally and professionally, and to apply this knowledge as you conduct your search and as you evaluate job offers.

- **Setting your career solidly on a path toward your long-term goals.** This is a pivotal time and one that allows you to pursue your career vision and offers you exposure and experience that can increase your professional stature.

- **Increasing your short- and long-term income potential.** This is a good time to research compensation in your profession and industry and see where you stand. Then you can consider what professional development – if any – you need to increase your income.

- **Learning to manage your career better.** Many of the techniques used in career transition have long-term value in managing your career better. By learning them now, you increase your odds of getting more of what you want – and less of what you do not want – in your work life in the future.

The Emotional Side of Career Transition

During this time of transition, you may experience any combination of reactions: shock, denial, anger, sadness, guilt, anxiety, fear, relief, and maybe even excitement. Any normal person can expect to experience at least a few of these. Some of them are more acute at the beginning of a search; however, it is important to understand that some or all of them may occur throughout your search project.

Some of our candidates have described search as a roller coaster ride; others as a bungee cord jump. Suffice it to say, it is a time of incredible lows and equally incredible highs. Here are some interim strategies:

- **Stay positive.** Do not panic. Your life is changing, not ending. And that change may just lead to a more satisfying work situation.

- **Think of yourself as having a new job now** rather than as being jobless. Your new job is managing your job search project, and it is a very important next step in your career. It will use all of your skills and experience – and may be an opportunity to develop new ones.

- **Be easy on yourself.** This can happen to anyone – and has happened to almost everyone. Take care of your physical, mental and emotional health. Reward yourself, give yourself permission to do pleasurable things and do what you need to do to handle the stress.

- **Do not keep your search a secret –** especially from your family and those close to you. The more secretive you are, the harder it will be for anyone to assist you. On the other hand, do not get on the phone immediately and tell all of your professional colleagues about your situation. Take the time to get yourself – and your communications strategy – together so that when you do talk to people you are prepared and effective.

- **Refrain from criticizing** your former company, boss or colleagues – especially when you are talking to prospective employers or other contacts. This will always work against you because it raises questions about how well (or poorly) you deal with difficult situations.

- **Stay in the moment, stay busy.** Do not isolate yourself. Look around you. How many other people do you know who have been in this same situation? Talk to them, share your feelings and ask how they worked through them.

Your Search Project Needs to be Managed

Job search needs to be managed just as you would a work-related or personal project. It includes definable stages, delineated steps and identifiable milestones.

During your career, you have probably been involved in the management of numerous work-related projects. In your personal life, perhaps you have planned a party or a wedding, a vacation trip or even a new custom-built home.

You know from these experiences that effective project management involves definable phases, delineated steps and identifiable milestones. Managing a project as important as your job search needs to be structured in the same manner. These materials help you do that.

Most managers and professionals have acquired project management skills during their careers. However, many do not recognize the need to use them in job search because they do not view search as work, much less a project. This view can lead to reduced productivity and, as a result, a longer and more frustrating search.

The nature of search is such that most people encounter significant barriers to sustained high productivity.

Barriers to Productivity in Search

Most people in job search, especially people who do not take advantage of career transition services, are less productive in search than in their normal work.

Even individuals who have been exposed to professional career transition services in the past might experience a downturn in productivity. In one large study, two-thirds of the unemployed respondents reported that they spent five hours or less in search-related activities each week. Why are people so unproductive in an activity as important as finding a good new job?

Part of the problem is that involuntary termination, unemployment and the search itself nearly always create barriers to productivity. Some barriers to productivity can be individually addressed, but others are simply part of the landscape of search during a period of unemployment.

One of the first barriers you may need to overcome are the myths out there. Some people in job search might even use these myths as "crutches" or excuses for not putting their full effort into finding a new job. If you're serious about finding a job, you need to realize the truth about these tales. Don't believe everything you hear. Here are some examples:

I can't get a job if I don't have one. People don't give up on this one easily. It's simply not true that no one out of work can get hired because only people who are working get hired. LHH candidates dispel this belief all the time as they see those around them getting prospects and jobs – and then they confidently go forth and land.

I'm too old to get hired. There are three components of age – chronological age, skill set and the impression you make. If your skill set is up to date in your field and you appear enthusiastic and young at heart, age won't matter.

I can't get hired at that company because they just downsized. Companies need to adjust their staffing as business conditions change. Sometimes there is a need for new employees in one department at the same time as changing conditions require a cutback in another department. If both departments use the same skill sets, people can be moved from one area to another. But if different skills are required, the company will hire in one area while doing a layoff in another.

I have no experience in that industry – I can't get hired there. This is not always true. Sometimes less-qualified candidates get hired because of their "fit" with a company. In addition to your specific background, you're selling enthusiasm, intelligence, motivation and interest in them.

There are no jobs in the summer or over the holidays. Schools may take a break during the summer, but employers certainly don't. Holiday periods where hiring slows down are always great opportunities to network and position yourself for the jobs that open up after the holiday. So don't pay attention to those who say "There are no jobs out there – especially now" or "Everyone is away for the summer."

It is important to be aware of all the possible barriers at the outset so that you are not taken by surprise by them later on. The exercise on the following page may help you realize and understand your barriers.

Congratulations to you for already taking the pro-active step of adding job search structure, expertise and skills by going through this program.

What Are Your Barriers to Productivity?

This exercise is designed to evaluate what might hinder your progress in job search. Review each of these possible barriers. Check the boxes next to the scenarios that might fit your personal situation.

☐ **Lack of job search expertise.** Some people do not know what needs to be done or how to do it. Even those aware of the overall activities needed may not be certain about the steps required to complete them.

☐ **Lack of search skills.** Lacking some of the skills required to conduct an effective search, or pursuing the wrong jobs or wrong employers, may result in low productivity.

☑ **Lack of an effective plan.** Winging it day-to-day without a plan to guide and prioritize your activities or following an unsound plan will not get you where you want to go.

☑ **Emotional stress (such as depression, anger or anxiety).** These feelings are natural but can become a barrier to an effective search when not properly managed. In search, repeated rejection can often lead to depression and ensuing inactivity.

☑ **Avoidance behavior.** Avoiding distasteful search activities or feelings of rejection by engaging in more pleasant busy work, such as searching Internet job boards or passively waiting for a company to make the next move, can hinder moving proactively toward goals.

☐ **Shifts in relationships.** Former friends may not return phone calls. Former colleagues may not know how to relate to people who have lost their jobs.

☐ **Lowered self-esteem and confidence.** Feelings caused by job loss or rejection in the search process can make it difficult to maintain self-confidence and productivity.

☑ **Lack of time structure.** Jobs are usually heavily structured (regular work hours and deadlines). In job search, individuals must manage their own time.

☐ **Lack of organizational structure, support and resources.** Even with the resources provided by Lee Hecht Harrison, job search is still primarily more of an individual and entrepreneurial activity than corporate employment.

☐ **The rejection cycle.** Repeated rejection is a fact of life in search. Since in the end you accept only one offer and everything before that does not work out, the entire search, by definition, may be seen as nothing but rejection. This can engender the common cycle of rejection, depression and inactivity that often undermines search productivity.

Use CRN to Help in Your Search

The Career Resource Network (CRN) is Lee Hecht Harrison's proprietary website designed to assist you in virtually all areas of your search. Access the site by logging into Career.lhh.com.
The CRN contains even more information and powerful tools to augment the material found in *Managing Your Search Project – The Blended Learning Version.* The CRN also provides additional material on topics such as Entrepreneurship and Retirement. You'll want to integrate the use of the CRN into your job search project. Here's just some of what the CRN provides:

CRN Link	Information	Milestones
Getting Started	Essential information when you're just beginning a job search on financial issues, emotional barriers and common myths. Also find links to your Unemployment Office and a short overview of what's ahead in your job search project.	1, 2
The Milestones	Includes the 10 Milestones that are a part of LHH's successful career transition model. We suggest you progress though each in order – and refer back as needed.	All
Resumes & Letters	A complete communications suite with more than 600 sample resumes, cover letters and email samples. Accomplishment, exit and positioning statement examples. Marketing plan templates. A "how-to" guide on posting your resume.	3-8
Online Strategies	Important information on setting up your online profiles, protecting your online brand, using Internet job boards, blogging and more. Also focuses on social networking on LinkedIn, Facebook, Twitter and other sites.	All
Job Search	Effective networking, interviewing and negotiating strategies. How to identify and work with recruiters, and find and use job leads.	5-10
Learning Center	A range of downloadable media, including podcasts, interviews and video presentations. Self-paced e-learning courses and listings of on-site events and webinars you can participate in.	All
Blogs and News	The latest on social media trends. Topical news information on current job market and economic issues from authoritative sources. Tips to assist you in your search.	All

Use CRN to Explore Career Direction

Some people take the opportunity while they are "between positions" to do some self-assessment, to consider major changes in their careers or industries, and to sort out various career alternatives.

Job search is an opportunity to explore career options, and you may find that you have more than you thought. If there is anything about the direction of your career that you'd like to change, this could be your chance to do it. This is certainly a good time to take stock of where you are in life.

You have options in what kind of work you decide to do next and in where you choose to do it. The "where" part includes industry and kind of organization as well as geographic location. Sometimes the culture of the organization where you work is as important to job satisfaction as what you do every day.

You can certainly pursue finding a job while exploring other career options. They're actually a good combination, as one will often shed light on the other.

You also may want to examine if your career is in high demand. If not, you might consider one of the growing career fields such as technology or healthcare. See the Career Resource Network (CRN) for more.

The Entrepreneurship Route

Who hasn't entertained the notion of being self-employed? Who hasn't sometimes dreamed of being one's own boss, of owning a business and building it successfully?

If this is your decision, the CRN can guide you through specifics of this process with 36 different milestones.

The Retirement Decision

Another option possibly open to you is that of an active retirement. Retirement today is far different from what we may have witnessed with our parents and grandparents. In fact, many experts believe that the "R" word should itself be retired, since it no longer applies to most people entering this new, productive, and vibrant stage of their lives.

Whether you are approaching traditional retirement age or not, you might benefit from reviewing contemporary retirement options. You also can find these on the CRN with a six milestone process.

No matter what path you choose, LHH and its resources will help you find your way.

Assess opportunity

Plan your search

Assess Opportunity

Assessing Opportunity and planning your search include Milestones 1 through 4. Milestones 2, 3 and 4 together comprise the marketing plan.

As with any successful project, the time spent properly preparing pays dividends in time saved later and in better results. Tracking your progress in this phase involves using a simple completion checklist found in the Search Project Organizer, which can be found on the Career Resource Network (CRN).

Milestone	Outcome	Pages
1. Survey Your Professional Environment	**You are able to summarize the current state of your profession and industry,** including the key trends shaping the future and how these trends will directly affect your career goals.	3 - 8
2. Determine Your Professional Objective	**You can state your professional objective in a phrase or sentence** so the kind of work you are seeking is clearly understood by people inside and outside your profession.	9 - 26
3. Create Your Communications Strategy	**You have a communications strategy that is appropriate to your professional objective** and appealing to hiring managers in your target market. It is reflected in an effectively written positioning statement, exit statement, accomplishment stories and resume.	27 - 58
4. Define Your Target Market	**You have established clear criteria for the group of organizations you plan to pursue** (geographic boundaries, industries, size of companies and preferred organizational culture), and researched and prepared a prioritized target list of 50 organizations you will pursue initially.	59-68

Milestone 1

Survey Your Professional Environment

Why this Milestone is Important...

Educating yourself on your professional environment – keeping updated on the latest and potential future trends and developments in your field – makes you a more appealing candidate when you speak with hiring managers because you are able to better discuss what is happening or could happen in your particular profession.

This research also creates a context for your search by allowing you to get beyond the confines of your last employer, clarify exactly which job titles are best for you and gauge where you stand in relationship to your profession as a whole. Continuing to stay updated on what is happening in your professional environment after you are reemployed is also just good career management.

Survey Your Industry Environment As Well

While surveying your professional environment, you also may want to look at your industry environment, which might include one industry or many. Being aware of your industry environment also adds to your appeal as a candidate because it helps you discuss with hiring managers how your professional expertise fits into their particular industries.

An Integrated, Ongoing Process

There is no need to complete this survey of your professional and industry environments before you begin other elements of your search. In fact, it is usually better to integrate this research work with other activities and the completion of other milestones.

You can, for example, research industries and specific companies within them at the same time. Later, when you are talking to contacts about certain organizations, you may also find the opportunity to discuss industries, your profession and the larger issues affecting both.

Questions to Explore

- *What current major trends are affecting my industry? What might the future trends be?*

- *What are the major trends currently affecting my profession? How has my profession changed? How might it change in the future?*

- *How are these changes affecting the competencies required for success now and in the future?*

- *What are the hot topics in my field that I should be able to address to remain competitive?*

- *What are some of the new career opportunities created by the changes in my industry and profession?*

- *What emerging issues do I find most interesting?*

Suggested Actions

- **Read articles about current problems, issues or developments affecting your profession.** Review some that provide a broad overview, but focus on those that interest you the most.

- **Read articles published over the past 12 months on your industry and the trends affecting it.** If you are considering moving to another industry, read about that one as well.

- **Search the Internet for information on your profession and industry to identify relevant trends, such as the impact of green jobs.** Check industry, company, financial and professional association websites for the latest information.

- **Join social networking sites** or any of the emerging "niche" sites for any information that your contacts may provide.

- **Look for recent books in the local library or bookstore about your industry and profession** to gain an understanding of the larger business trends that are affecting your type of work. Read the jackets and skim the introductions. Then pick a book that intrigues you and read it.

- **Write a brief analysis of the profession and industry in which you plan to work.** Include the key trends, likely challenges and emerging opportunities.

Defining Your Profession and How You Fit In

Before you begin to survey your professional environment, it is important that you have effectively defined your profession. What is it that you really do? Does your current job title actually describe your profession?

Perhaps your last job title was that of a senior analyst. That job title may not mean much outside of your former work environment. After all, there is no profession called senior analyst. A senior analyst could be in the profession of economics, politics or strategic planning.

Defining your profession begins with an examination of your work experience and expertise. If your past experience does not fit clearly into a professional category, ask yourself these questions:

- *What would my ideal work be? What profession is it in?*

- *What are my passions? What professions do they suggest?*

- *What comes naturally to me? What professions do they suggest?*

The Changing Job Market

Why do you need a clear definition of your profession? Because the job market, indeed the world, is constantly changing, and may have changed significantly since you were last in career transition. Organizations have had to change to compete more successfully in the global marketplace. They have become leaner and more focused on productivity, and they are insisting on a workforce that is agile and resilient. You need to know what effect this constantly changing job market is having on your profession.

The Effect of Technology

The technological cutting edge keeps moving and has affected virtually every profession in some tangible way. New skills are expected, and old skills are evolving around new technologies. You need to know what impact technology is having on your profession.

Your Profession and the Marketplace

Every industry or organization requires certain professions to achieve its goals. You need to know what your profession means in the marketplace you are about to enter, particularly if you are contemplating changing industries. This means looking at your profession and making some decisions about your future work life and the types of companies and industries that interest you and need your professional expertise.

Here are some ways you can do this:

1. Review your work history and the profession(s) in which you have worked.

2. Explore advertised positions, in print and on the Internet, particularly looking at industry and profession profiles. Some Internet sites have "real people" profiles that give you a glimpse of professions within industries.

3. Find information on the Internet for your profession by using online occupational handbooks. They describe working conditions, training and education requirements, earnings and expected job prospects.

4. Ask friends, colleagues, previous customers and other LHH candidates what profession they see you pursuing in the future.

5. Review associations that you have joined or want to join.

Questions to ask about your profession

- *How viable is my profession? Will it become obsolete?*

- *What is the probable length of time I can continue to work in my profession?*

- *What are the compensation ranges of my profession?*

- *What continuing education and training is required in my profession?*

Surveying Your Professional Environment

Once you have truly defined your profession in terms of what you do and where you want to do it, you need to educate yourself on the latest developments in your profession and your professional environment.

Research and read articles about your profession to familiarize yourself with the current trends. The Internet is a valuable tool for researching information, associations and experts in your field. Most professional journals have websites. Skimming articles online is a good way to pick up the latest jargon in your profession.

Guidelines for Surveying Your Professional Environment

- **Study the classifieds in newspapers and online job postings.** Note all the companies and industries that need your professional services.

- **Read industry newsletters and professional journals,** regularly check out articles in your local and national newspapers and research relevant websites. Use the information you discover to generate more questions and to share in your conversations.

- **When you are further along in your preparation** and are gathering marketplace information and beginning to get your message out, develop sources – people with whom you can discuss your findings about your professional environment.

- **Talk to professional organizations and to general contacts on the phone.** It is a highly productive way to get the information you need.

Tips and Techniques

Complete Your Preparation Before Using Your Network

Talking to people is an important component of the work of this milestone, but you need to be sure you are prepared before having these conversations. Your exit and positioning statements (see Milestone 3) are particularly important. It is a good idea to complete all of your work on creating a communications strategy prior to using your network to make sure you make the best possible impression. Although it is important to begin work on Milestone 1 now, many people find they can more effectively complete it by combining it with Milestone 5, Gather Marketplace Information.

Productivity Pointer

Collect and Organize Useful Information on Web

Begin now to build files (both electronic and hard copy) of articles on your profession and on each of the industries that interest you, and continue to collect these throughout your search. Bookmark relevant websites so that you can return to them easily. You sometimes will find occasions to share this useful information with your contacts, perhaps even helping them solve a problem. Reviewing this information prior to an interview might make you the best informed and most up-to-date candidate. It also will help you better manage your career after you find new employment.

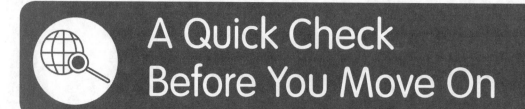

A Quick Check Before You Move On

Now that you're in search, you need to be more up-to-date on what's happening in your profession or industry than ever before. Surveying your professional environment will get you informed about the key trends shaping your industry's future, and how these trends may directly affect your career goals.

There are three good reasons for undertaking a survey of your professional environment:

1. **You'll be a smarter candidate when you speak with hiring managers** because you will be able to better discuss what is happening or could happen in your industry or profession. You'll have opinions and points-of-view that will make you a more knowledgeable candidate and distinguish you from others.

2. **It could shorten your search.** The more you know about developments in your industry and profession, the better you'll be able to put together a good target list of organizations that could use your skills. You'll be able to eliminate organizations that don't match up with the facts you uncovered and the criteria you developed, and you'll add others that now measure up.

3. **It might save you from pursuing a position in a profession or industry that's marked for extinction,** or an industry that's changing fundamentally – in its product line, locale, or composition. You may wind up reexamining many of your current perceptions based on your information.

Before you leave this milestone:

- Make sure you've registered for the Career Resource Network (CRN). Upon starting your program, you should have received an email with your registration ID to access the site.

- Go to CRN and analyze the state of your current profession and industry with information from the databases available to you, including financial and professional association websites.

- Check out the downloadable podcasts and e-learning modules on this milestone on CRN. They are available to you to review at your own pace, 24/7.

- Begin to network with your former colleagues and with new people you meet. Join or revisit work-oriented social networking sites for information that your contacts there may provide.

- Begin to examine blogs on Twitter that pertain to your industry. It will help you discover current trends as well as where your industry is headed in the future.

Milestone 2

Determine Your Professional Objective

Why this Milestone is Important...

Every project begins with an overall goal or objective. In search, the most obvious goal is to find a great new job. However, you need to clearly convey exactly what kind of work you are seeking.

A Professional Objective Defines What You Want to Do

A professional objective defines the kind of work you want to do within your profession, making it easier for the people you talk with to know exactly what it is you are looking for and be of optimal assistance to you. If you are a human resources professional, for instance, it is important to let people know what kind of human resources position you are looking for (e.g., recruiting, compensation and benefits).

Perhaps the most important reason for thinking through your professional objective is that it is a reflection of you and where you want your career and your work life to go next. People sometimes start this process by considering their mission or purpose in life and where work fits into that mission.

The next step is to create a vision of where you would like your work life to be in three or five years. Your professional objective is an abbreviated statement, a definition, of the immediate next step toward materializing that vision.

Getting to that definition involves conducting a self-assessment of your skills, interests, values and personal preferences. This self-assessment is a major – and necessary – component if you are to create a professional objective that clearly defines the kind of work you will be happiest doing.

A Professional Objective Gives Direction to Your Search

Expending effort on this milestone early on in your search is time well spent and will actually save you time in the long term. A professional objective focuses and gives direction to your search by enabling you to clarify for yourself, and then clearly communicate to others, exactly what it is you are seeking. Your professional objective sets the tone and direction for your communications strategy and is the premise from which you create your resume. Sometimes it is included as a separate entity at the top of a resume or incorporated into the summary statement.

A Professional Objective Is at the Core of Your Marketing Plan

Having a well thought out marketing plan is just as important in a search project as it is in launching a new product. Companies often spend millions of dollars creating and executing marketing plans when launching new products. They do this because they know that this kind of up-front investment in time and money means a more rapid product launch with potentially higher sales. In job search, your personal marketing plan serves a similar purpose. (Creating your personal marketing plan is covered in detail in the chapter for Milestone 4.)

Your professional objective is at the core of your own personal marketing plan. It positions you in the market by letting people know what kind of work you are seeking. It can make the difference between a slow, meandering search and a rapid, focused one.

Why this Milestone is Important...

A Professional Objective Is an Opportunity to Explore Your Options

A professional objective needs to go beyond your last job title. A well-developed professional objective presents you with an opportunity to broaden and explore your options more fully – to look at new possibilities that may offer a better, more satisfying fit than your last job title.

To enable you to explore your options fully, your professional objective needs to be realistic. A common objection to having a professional objective is that it will limit options. The truth is that you want a realistic professional objective that, if need be, excludes inappropriate possibilities and is consistent with your qualifications. It makes no sense to explore opportunities for which no one will see you as qualified.

A Professional Objective Should Be Easily Understood and Focused

Your professional objective also needs to be consistent with marketplace standards and commonly used language. Using language understood only within your industry or by your last employer to describe your objective is not a good idea. Think about your most recent job title. Is it so esoteric as to be totally obscure in the marketplace? Public Relations Manager is a clearly understood title. A Level Two Technical Coordinator is not. Be sure you use language that is generally used and understood.

Your professional objective needs to be sufficiently focused – not too broad or too narrow. An objective that is too broadly stated (I am looking for a management position) can be vague and may lead to a wandering, unproductive search.

On the other hand, an objective that is too narrowly stated (I am looking for a position as an incentive compensation analyst) can cost you months of looking for jobs that exist in such small numbers that there is little chance of finding one.

The good news is that you do not need to have a perfect professional objective to get started. You can begin by describing a broad area, then refine your objective as you talk to people, write your resume or complete your marketing plan.

 Tips and Techniques

Using Umbrella Terms

Listed below are some of the more common umbrella terms useful in creating professional objectives. Terms such as these often can be used as the first words in a professional objective.

- Senior management
- General management (P&L)
- Financial services/management
- Information technology/management
- Public relations
- Human resources/management
    - Recruiting
    - Compensation
    - Compliance
- Legal
- Sales/management
- Manufacturing/operations management
- Marketing/management
    - Product management
    - Advertising
    - Market research

Questions to Explore

- *What are my interests? What do I really enjoy doing? What type of activity or environment attracts me?*

- *What do I do best? What are three to six of my strongest skills or competencies? What differentiates me from others seeking similar work?*

- *What are my values and priorities? What is important to me? How does work fit in with other aspects of my life?*

- *What would my ideal job look like? What do I want my life and work to look like five years from now?*

- *How would I describe my management style or my personality? How do they fit with my professional objective?*

- *All things considered, is my professional objective realistic?*

Suggested Actions

- **Generate a list of options that interest you,** listing everything you have thought about doing now and in the future. Share the list with people who know you well and ask for their reactions.

- **Assess your personal interests, values, skills and preferences** so that they are reflected in your professional objective.

- **Confirm your self-assessment by talking to two or three people you trust** and who know you well and ask them for relevant and honest feedback.

- **Join or visit work-related social networking sites** or any of the emerging "niche" sites for perspectives that your contacts may provide on your self-assessment.

- **Consider other career alternatives** as a way of determining how you might transfer your skills into other functions or industries.

- **Talk with a knowledgeable person, such as a professional career consultant,** to confirm your overall career direction and immediate professional objective.

- **Create a career vision** of what you want your work life to be like in three to five years. An immediate professional objective is usually best planned in the context of a long-term personal vision of your career.

- **If you are considering entrepreneurship or ecopreneurship,** investigate this path carefully and assess how well your skills, interests and values support that career direction. You may want to continue your job search while exploring self-employment.

- **Write down your work-related accomplishments** so that you can clearly identify your skills and traits, identify potential markets and present yourself well.

- **Draft a sentence or a phrase** that concisely describes the kind of work you are seeking. This will become your professional objective.

Assessing Yourself

Your professional objective needs to reflect who you are and what is important to you, such as your skills, competencies, personal characteristics, interests and values, as well as your overall experience.

Your first step to creating an objective that reflects who you are is to conduct your own self-assessment. This ensures that the direction you choose is a good fit for you and that you are seen as qualified. Your work history and accomplishments are an excellent starting point for this assessment.

The results of this self-assessment will also help you see more clearly what career options are possible for you – using different combinations of your strengths.

When your overall career direction is clear, you can write a brief and effective professional objective that summarizes the kind of work you want in the immediate future. This statement will be the basis of your resume, marketing plan and job search.

As you prepare your professional objective, you will also accumulate material you will need to promote yourself as a well-qualified candidate. In resumes and interviews – as in product marketing – your product's strengths and potential benefits must be clear.

The following exercises are designed to assist you in conducting a self-assessment leading to a professional objective. It will also lay the groundwork for you to promote yourself effectively in your chosen target market.

Three Key Areas to Assess

The following are the key areas to assess in making a sound career decision. They are organized under three basic questions:

1. **WHAT DO YOU DO BEST?**

   Your skills, knowledge and competencies. These are acquired through education and experience of all kinds (such as employment, volunteer work, life experience) and represent your principal assets in your job market. Correctly labeling skills is an important part of communicating your value.

   Your personal characteristics. These characteristics are inborn or developed early in life. They can include abilities, talents or a predisposition to certain career directions.

2. **WHAT DO YOU LIKE TO DO?**

   Your interests. Your professional objective should be something you are interested in as well as something you are good at. After all, life is more pleasant when you do things you truly enjoy. You are also more likely to succeed when the work interests you.

3. **WHAT ARE YOUR PRIORITIES IN LIFE?**

   Your values. These are your core beliefs about what is most and least important in life. They usually evolve slowly and may have changed since you last made major career decisions.

   Your personal preferences. Your professional objective should be consistent with your career vision and lifestyle needs (including location, schedule and income).

   Your motivations. These are the drives or needs that propel you along in your chosen career direction. With high motivation, you move rapidly in your career but you may make sacrifices elsewhere in your life.

What is a Skill?

To answer questions about your skills, you need to know what your skills are in very specific terms. Most people cannot describe their skills off the top of their heads and have to do some careful skill analysis.

Assessing Your Skills

There are three kinds of things to remember when you are asked about your skills:

1. **THINGS YOU CAN DO**
   Employers want to know the specific actions you can take, such as "organize an effective presentation" or "develop a project timeline."

2. **THINGS YOU KNOW**
   Jobs require knowledge as well as skills. Employers want to know if you know the essentials for the job.

3. **ROLES YOU PLAY**
   Employers want to know how you can combine skills, knowledge and personal characteristics to fulfill particular workplace roles.

The exercises on the following pages are designed to help you identify your skills by analyzing your accomplishments at work. The first step is to identify accomplishments. The second step is to flesh out the story of each accomplishment and see what skills you used.

 Tips and Techniques
If you are struggling with identifying some of your skills, stop, take a deep breath and think about what you are proudest of in your career. What excited you the most? Write down the story and then go back and identify the skills and competencies you used that made it successful. You might be surprised at what you find. It also becomes one of your first accomplishment stories!

Identifying Accomplishments

This exercise is designed to help you identify your accomplishments at work. Review the questions and place a check next to those that apply to you. Beside each item you check, specify a key word that will remind you of the accomplishment. Each accomplishment is an indicator of one or more skills in action. Later you will name these skills. You also will use accomplishments to communicate your value in your resume and when interviewing.

Accomplishments	Key Word
❏ Did you identify a problem and solve it? What were the results?	_____
❏ Did you introduce a new system or procedure that made work easier or more accurate?	_____
❏ Did you save the company money or time? How much? What positive impact did the savings have on the company?	_____
❏ Did your efforts increase the company's profit line? By how much?	_____
❏ Did you increase productivity or reduce downtime? By how much? How did the savings affect the bottom line?	_____
❏ Did you effectively manage systems or people? What were the results of your efforts?	_____
❏ Did you initiate a sales or incentive program that worked? What were the results in dollars and cents? On company image? On morale?	_____
❏ Did you participate in decision making or planning? What contributions did you make to the team? What were the results of your efforts?	_____
❏ Did you write any major reports, programs, publications, promotions or newsletters? What was the intended audience? What was the distribution or readership?	_____
❏ Did you improve the efficiency of people or operations? What were the savings?	_____
❏ Were you responsible for reducing staff or trimming an operation? How were you able to do this efficiently?	_____
❏ Were you involved in a start-up or shutdown? What were the challenges you faced?	_____
❏ Did you automate or create systems or procedures? How many people did you train? How much money was involved in the automation?	_____
❏ Were you a liaison between departments? How were you able to make things run more efficiently?	_____
❏ Did you produce reports or data that enabled management to make more informed decisions?	_____

How Accomplishments Identify Skills

In today's job market, it is important to know your skills and be able to find positions that require those skills. You might want (or need) to transfer your skills into other functional areas or industries. Knowing your skills will help you to identify potential markets and communicate your value to a potential employer.

Skills Identified through Accomplishments

When you are successful, it is usually because you are applying your skills and because your personal traits are assets for the task at hand. An analysis of your achievements, accomplishments and successes, therefore, can lead to a clear definition of these skills and traits. This analysis enables you to identify recurring patterns or themes.

In this exercise, you will analyze your most important work-related achievements. You may use those you identified in the preceding exercise. Also, fill in what skills or personal characteristics you used in each accomplishment.

Situation — Describe the situation	Obstacles — Describe the obstacles you faced	Actions — List the actions you took	Results — Describe the results you helped obtain
1.			
Skills Used:			
2.			
Skills Used:			

Situation Describe the situation	Obstacles Describe the obstacles you faced	Actions List the actions you took	Results Describe the results you helped obtain
3.			
Skills Used:			
4.			
Skills Used:			
5.			
Skills Used:			

S ituation	Describe the situation.
O bstacles	Describe the obstacles you faced.
A ctions	List the actions you took.
R esults	Describe the results you helped obtain and the benefits to your employer.

Developing Your Accomplishment Stories

The technique you used on the preceding pages is what we call SOAR. It is an excellent guide for developing accomplishment stories that showcase your skills. In an interview, your SOAR answer provides specific information on the situation, obstacles, action and results. The SOAR acronym is easy to remember and will help you organize material in interview situations.

Your SOAR stories put your accomplishments in a business context that an employer can understand.

Suppose an interviewer asked the following question:

Describe a time you beat out the competition by capitalizing on a marketplace trend?

Your SOAR response might be:

"I was the product manager at Exceptional Pet Foods for its "large breeds" dog products. Exceptional faced tough competition from national brands that outspent us in advertising and promotional efforts, and we were losing market share to them, particularly in supermarkets.

"I conducted market analysis and customer interviews that indicated an opportunity for a lower-priced line in bulk packaging to be sold exclusively through warehouse and outdoor stores. The idea was to appeal to consumers who loved their dogs, but didn't want to spend top dollar on them.

"We introduced the Mega-Dog line in 2011, and it quickly established itself in those outlets. Mega-Dog now accounts for more than one-third of Exceptional's dog food revenues and was profitable within its second year on the market."

The SOAR approach works because it …

- presents a complete story, from the context through to the results
- is applicable outside your industry – shows your thinking process.

You should have as many as 10-20 SOAR stories ready when you go in for an interview. You probably won't need that many, but you never know what the interviewer might ask. These SOAR stories are great for open-ended questions.

Practice the SOAR Technique

Think about the following sample questions and consider how you might answer them using the SOAR technique. Practice delivering your answers out loud, so you're confident when you face the interviewer.

1. Tell me how your background qualifies you for this position?

2. What important career goals did you set and reach on your last job?

3. Tell me about a time when you used your education and training?

4. Tell me about a time you were not successful in adapting to change?

Transferable Skills Inventory

Use this list to assist you in identifying the skills you have learned or developed through experience. Select the six skills that best describe you. Place a check next to each skill. Be sure each skill you select is supported by experience, education or achievements. This list is necessarily general. It is important that you include any additional skills needed to create an accurate picture of yourself.

COMMUNICATING
- ❑ Corresponding
- ❑ Editing
- ❑ Interviewing
- ❑ Managing conflict
- ❑ Negotiating
- ❑ Public speaking
- ❑ Writing
- ❑ Drawing
- ❑ Facilitating
- ❑ Listening
- ❑ Mediating
- ❑ Presenting ideas
- ❑ Relating to customers
- ❑ Other: _____

COORDINATING
- ❑ Cataloging
- ❑ Following up
- ❑ Scheduling
- ❑ Correcting
- ❑ Reporting
- ❑ Other: _____

DEVELOPING PEOPLE
- ❑ Assessing performance
- ❑ Counseling
- ❑ Helping others
- ❑ Teaching
- ❑ Training
- ❑ Coaching
- ❑ Developing
- ❑ Motivating
- ❑ Team building
- ❑ Other: _____

FINANCIAL MANAGEMENT
- ❑ Auditing
- ❑ Controlling
- ❑ Financial analysis
- ❑ Fund raising
- ❑ Budgeting
- ❑ Cost accounting
- ❑ Financial planning
- ❑ Other: _____

MANAGING DATA
- ❑ Analyzing data
- ❑ Computing
- ❑ Managing information
- ❑ Research
- ❑ Taking inventory
- ❑ Assessing quality
- ❑ Gathering data
- ❑ Measuring
- ❑ Setting standards
- ❑ Other: _____

MANAGING/DIRECTING
- ❑ Approving
- ❑ Developing procedures
- ❑ Directing
- ❑ Implementing
- ❑ Interpreting policy
- ❑ Managing people
- ❑ Managing tasks
- ❑ Other: _____
- ❑ Delegating
- ❑ Developing systems
- ❑ Formulating
- ❑ Instructing
- ❑ Making decisions
- ❑ Managing projects
- ❑ Revitalizing

ORGANIZING
- ❑ Administering
- ❑ Categorizing
- ❑ Projecting
- ❑ Setting priorities
- ❑ Assigning
- ❑ Developing work plans
- ❑ Restructuring
- ❑ Other: _____

PLANNING
- ❑ Analyzing
- ❑ Designing
- ❑ Developing strategy
- ❑ Surveying
- ❑ Conceptualizing
- ❑ Developing policy
- ❑ Reviewing
- ❑ Other: _____

SELLING/MARKETING
- ❑ Advertising
- ❑ Managing sales
- ❑ Pricing
- ❑ Relating to clients
- ❑ Writing proposals
- ❑ Analyzing markets
- ❑ Marketing
- ❑ Promoting
- ❑ Selling
- ❑ Other: _____

SERVING
- ❑ Client relations
- ❑ Responding promptly
- ❑ Handling complaints
- ❑ Other: _____

TECHNICAL SKILLS
- ❑ Computer literate
- ❑ Designing systems
- ❑ Engineering
- ❑ Scientific research
- ❑ Programming
- ❑ Designing
- ❑ Developing products
- ❑ Inventing
- ❑ Manufacturing
- ❑ Other: _____

Assessing Your Personal Characteristics

Each of us possesses certain personal characteristics – or traits that make us unique and enhance our ability to perform different tasks successfully. To help determine your personal characteristics, follow the three steps in this exercise. After you are done, you may wish to confirm your personal assessment with a friend.

1. Review the list below and select the six traits that describe you best. Check the box next to each. Be sure that there is clear evidence of your accomplishments for the traits you check.

2. Of these six that you checked, circle the three that represent your most prominent traits.

3. Now look for any traits that an interviewer might consider a weakness. Put an 'X' next to those traits.

☐ Accurate	☐ Efficient	☐ Kind	☐ Responsible
☐ Adventurous	☐ Emotional	☐ Leader	☐ Responsive
☐ Artistic	☐ Energetic	☐ Levelheaded	☐ Self-assured
☐ Assertive	☐ Entertaining	☐ Loyal	☐ Self-controlled
☐ Challenging	☐ Enthusiastic	☐ Original	☐ Self-starter
☐ Civic-minded	☐ Expressive	☐ People-oriented	☐ Sense of humor
☐ Committed	☐ Good attitude	☐ Perfectionist	☐ Sensitive
☐ Communicate well	☑ Hard worker	☐ Personable	☐ Sociable
☐ Compassionate	High standards	☐ Persuasive	☐ Stable
☐ Confident	☐ Imaginative	☐ Physically fit	☐ Tolerant
☐ Creative	☐ Independent	☐ Practical	☑ Trustworthy
☐ Curious	☐ Inquisitive	☐ Productive	☐ Other: _____
☐ Dedicated	☐ Intelligent	☐ Rational	
☐ Dependable	☐ Intuitive		

Assessing Your Interests

The choices we make about work – no matter what field – are influenced by our interests. This exercise will help you assess your interests: the things you like and do not like to do.

Your interests are another important part of career decision making. One way to identify your interests is to think back on your career and determine what you liked and disliked about each of your jobs, starting with your most recent. Summarize your likes and dislikes below.

LIKES

_____

_____

_____

_____

DISLIKES

_____

_____

_____

_____

Assessing Your Competencies

Competencies are the clusters of skills and personal characteristics that work in concert to enable you to perform certain kinds of work effectively. Skills are what you can do; competencies are broader areas of expertise.

A simple example is a competency in word processing, which is composed of skills in the use of certain software, manual dexterity, spelling and grammar, combined with a personal ability to concentrate on printed material even in a room filled with noise and activity. A more complex example is leadership competencies, which may be defined differently in different organizations.

While a profession expects certain competencies, each individual in that profession is likely to have competencies that vary a bit from those expected. Organizations often speak of their core competencies – those that are central to accomplishing the work of the organization. For example, the competencies of a school could be education and child care.

If your personal competencies are relevant to the core competencies of the organization, you are more likely to be seen as important to the organization's future. People who understand how their competencies relate to their organization's mission become significant contributors and can create new opportunities for themselves.

In search, your ability to put your skills, knowledge and personality characteristics together into competencies relevant to those of your target organizations is an important part of your communication strategy.

Identifying competencies is not always easy. Your competencies must be important to the organization hiring you. It cannot simply be a function or a job title. Competencies describe your value beyond this year's needed skill.

To identify your competencies, start by considering:

- **What you do that no other person can do** quite the way you do it.

- **What your targeted employers will pay** a premium price for.

- **How you can set yourself apart** from others in your profession.

- **How you can maintain your career advantage** in the future.

Sample Competencies

Succession planning manager with:
- Strong analytical skills
- Expertise translating the big picture into specific business strategies
- Creativity to make the conceptual concrete and relevant

Marketing executive who creates sales results by:
- Accurate analysis of market trends
- Intuitive sense of market potential
- Planning marketing campaigns
- Assessing the impact on people

Technical leader who:
- Motivates to achieve goals in time of rapid market changes
- Demonstrates a track record that is practical, systematic and efficient
- Persuades and influences, in writing and public speaking

Corporate financial professional with skills in:
- Project management
- Departmental management
- International performance
- Budgeting
- Planning
- Communication
- Auditing

Assessing Your Personal Values

Taking the time and effort to discover what is valuable to you in life enables you to recognize internal guideposts that will help you make career decisions. Making value choices is not as easy. And, at times, values conflict.

Three Categories of Values

1. **Universal values -** We link our individual experiences with the rest of humanity. Universal values might be life, joy, love or peace.

2. **Cultural values -** We establish and maintain social order. Cultural values are reflected in language, status systems, education, government, law, economics and social institutions.

3. **Personal values -** Underlies the choices you make about your life and career. As adults grow older and accumulate life experience, their values often change. If you are 55, for example, your values may be quite different from those you had at 25. Your individual values are a result of individual temperament and experience. Re-examining your values can be an important part of making a successful career transition.

Number these values in order of importance with 1 being most important and 10 being least important. No ties allowed. If you add another value in the "other" category – make 11 the least important.

_____ **Independence and Autonomy:** Doing things on your own; not having too many rules and restrictions placed on you.

_____ **Power:** Controlling the situation around you in order to make things happen in organizations.

_____ **Leadership/Management:** Coordinating the work of others and taking responsibility for the overall results.

_____ **Technical Expertise:** Being strong in specific skill areas, such as finance, marketing, engineering or human resources.

_____ **Lifestyle:** Being holistic about unifying all of the various parts of your life, such as career, family and interests.

_____ **Service:** Contributing to the welfare of others; dedicating yourself to a worthwhile cause.

_____ **Friendship:** Being liked by others; maintaining important relationships and having companionship.

_____ **Security:** Reducing worries about future financial welfare; preferring stability and predictability.

_____ **Challenge:** Desiring to take on and win the "tough ones" in any field of endeavor.

_____ **Wealth:** Accumulating a large amount of money – more than average and much more than necessities require.

_____ **Other(s):**

What effect have your top three values had on your search?

My #1 Value: _____

Effect on Search _____

My #2 Value: _____

Effect on Search _____

My #3 Value: _____

Effect on Search _____

Creating Your Career Vision

An immediate professional objective is usually best formulated in the context of a long-term personal vision for your career. Where do you want to be in your work life in five years? Exactly what would you like your work situation to be? When you look at your life as a whole, what part do you want your career to play?

The clearer you are on this long-term vision, the more likely you are to move toward it in your next career step. Remember the process of creating a career vision requires keeping an open mind.

 ## Vision Statement

Five years from now, I will be leading a team of highly motivated, bottom-line-oriented people who have earned a reputation for being able to creatively and successfully tackle any problem presented to them. We will be recognized for making the company more profitable by garnering 10% more market share.

Write your vision of the career you would like to have. Some people find it useful to first think about their overall "life mission" or purpose – and even draft a mission statement – before defining a five-year vision.

Your Vision Statement:

Five years from now, I…

_____

_____

_____

_____

_____

_____

_____

Researching Job Titles

One of the outcomes of reorganizations and downsizing is that job titles have changed extensively.

As you work to determine your professional objective, you may need to identify the work you do by new and different descriptions. The key, of course, is being clear on what you do so that you will recognize it by whatever title your target organization may have chosen to label it.

As the economy has evolved and new business segments and functions have been created, the rigid nature of jobs and job titles has softened. In addition, reduced workforces have brought combinations and recombinations of job tasks and responsibilities. In almost every job category, people are being asked to work across traditional lines more than ever before. Job titles have struggled to keep up with these changes by being more descriptive and, at the same time, less precise.

Examples

Old Titles	New Titles
• Sales Manager	• Business Development Manager
• Human Resources Manager	• Human Capital Development Manager
• Customer Services	• Client Relations
• Director of Information Services	• Chief Information Officer

Identifying Core Competencies

The key then becomes identifying the core competencies required in your job function and searching for them rather than the imprecise job titles. In addition, having a good sense of where a particular job function or profession is headed (as you learned in Milestone 1) can be key to your current search and future career management.

Generic Titles for Managers

In writing professional objectives, managers are usually wise not to specify titles such as president, senior vice president or director, since these have widely varying definitions and compensation ranges. Some generic possibilities include:

Departmental Manager	Leads a team of specialized workers who share similar skills
Regional Manager	Manages a group of local managers
Senior Manager	Manages an entire functional area
General Manager/ Senior Executive	Provides overall leadership of a business unit, typically holding P & L responsibility

Setting Your Professional Objective

It is important to set goals before you take action. In your personal life, you probably know your destination before you leave on vacation. A professional objective provides the direction you need as you plan your search. It takes into consideration your values, skills, interests, personal characteristics and overall experience. It will set the tone for your resume and other communications.

It also will help you select and prioritize the targets of your search, since each professional objective fits best with certain segments of the job market.

The following exercise will help you develop a realistic and understandable professional objective.

Summarize Your Self-Assessment

All of the self-assessment material should be consistent with your professional objective. Your self-assessment may provide additional ideas for your professional objective, as well as provide an outline of material to support it.

Career Vision:

Skills and Competencies:	**Personal Characteristics:**
1.	1.
2	2.
3.	3.

Values:	**Interests:**
1.	1.
2	2.
3.	3.

Professional Objective:

Experience, education and key accomplishments supporting that professional objective:

A Quick Check Before You Move On

Crafting a good professional objective can take a little time, but it's a necessary step. After all, if you're not clear on what you're looking to do, how will you convince others that you're qualified and motivated to do it?

Your professional objective should...
1. establish your professional identity, while it...
2. identifies the position you're seeking, and...
3. summarizes your main qualifications in seeking it.

Here's an example that delivers on the three points above:

> **Vice President of Marketing in an organization where a strong track record of market share expansion and Internet savvy is needed.**

Your professional objective passes muster when the kind of work you are seeking is clearly understood by people inside and outside your profession. It's an important element in defining your personal and professional brand.

On page 60, we discuss a variation of the professional objective. This is called the 'professional objective with preferred functions', which you may prefer in developing your marketing plan.

Before you leave this milestone:
Go to Career Resource Network (CRN) to find the tools available there to assist you in completing the work of this milestone, such as:

- Self-assessment instruments
- E-learning on the subject and how to develop accomplishment stories using SOAR
- Samples of accomplishment statements
- Examples of job titles

If you're considering a move to another industry or career, you'll want to assess its current climate and prospects more thoroughly by using the databases available to you, including financial and professional association websites. Information on changing careers, entrepreneurship and an active retirement is available on CRN.

Milestone 3

Create Your Communications Strategy

Why this Milestone is Important...

Your communications strategy links your professional objective with your target market in language suitable to that market. Therefore, being able to create your communications strategy depends on the work you did determining your professional objective in Milestone 2 and, at least, a sense of your target market, although you may not yet have precisely defined it.

Professional Objective	Communications Strategy	Target Market
Describes what kind of work you want to do.	A well-crafted statement of what you have to offer. It is your message to the marketplace – your positioning statement.	Describes where you want to work.
Based on your skills, interests and values.	Presents your qualifications for the professional objective in ways hiring managers in the intended target market can relate to.	Lists organizations that may need the person described in professional objective.
Distinguishes you from the vast majority of others looking for work.	Distinguishes you from others with the same professional objective.	Defines the types of organizations in which you want to invest the most search time.

A Communications Strategy Presents an Overall Message to Your Target Market

The overall message is an outgrowth of your work on your professional objective and highlights your underlying skills, interests and values. The message needs to be presented in ways that appeal to the hiring managers as determined by your marketing plan. It needs to be both carefully crafted and authentic. The same message must be communicated in the resume, social media and in interviews. It also must be supported – or at least not contradicted – by your references. You must never say anything to undermine it.

A Communications Strategy Delivers a Consistent Message

Just as advertising repeats a single consistent message about a product, you must deliver a consistent message about yourself throughout your search. In fact, most people in search fall into a pattern of repeating the same message. Unfortunately, the message they choose to repeat has not always been carefully thought out. Because the average job hunter talks to more than 100 people, it is important that your message has been carefully crafted.

The starting point is your professional objective. But once people know you are a product manager (or financial manager or salesperson), they need to know what differentiates you from other product managers (or financial managers or salespeople). What kind of product manager are you? What are your unique strengths?

A Communications Strategy Links You to Your Likely Target Market

Your communications strategy needs to take into account the probable needs of your likely target market. What industry or industries will you pursue? What do they value? How does a product manager (or financial manager or salesperson) operate in that particular industry? Later, as you zero in on particular targets, think about the individual hiring managers to whom your message is directed. What do they value? What are they likely to need and want? Just as good advertising focuses on a particular target market, you need to focus your message on a particular audience. As you begin to talk to and interview with hiring managers, your focus will become even sharper.

Why this Milestone is Important...

A Communications Strategy Needs to Counteract Real or Perceived Deficits

No matter how good a candidate you are, there might be certain aspects of your background that some people perceive as deficits. A good communications strategy predicts as many real or perceived deficits as possible and incorporates an antidote to the objections into the original message. For example, a person concerned about being seen as too old might incorporate material on depth of experience or seasoned judgment into a communications strategy.

In marketing terms, these are all elements of positioning a product. As you would for a product you are marketing, you need to write a positioning statement for yourself that honestly puts forward your key competencies and unique strengths.

A Resume Reflects Your Communications Strategy

Once you have a sense of your communications strategy, you are ready to write a resume. Your resume, the interview and, for that matter, all conversations and emails in the course of a job search, need to reflect exactly the same communications strategy. Once you have formulated your strategy, you need to communicate a consistent message in many different ways to many different people.

The resume, like all communications, makes a case for why you are a good candidate for your stated professional objective. It is impossible to judge the quality of any resume without reference to a professional objective and a defined target market. What you need to say to get a job as a general manager of a $200 million business is completely different from what you need to say to get a job as a hospital social worker.

A resume is not a biography. It needs to cover just enough about you to make you a credible candidate – someone worth talking to about the stated professional objective. It must also conform closely enough to the conventions of resume writing so that it does not annoy readers or make them suspicious. For example, it must always include some kind of dated work history.

It is important to keep your target market in mind while completing your resume. Some people prefer to complete their entire marketing plan prior to beginning the resume. If you complete the resume prior to the marketing plan, you need to keep in mind your probable target market so that you can use the language of those targets and address what are likely to be their collective needs and wants.

Productivity Pointer

The core message of your communications strategy should include:

- A professional objective: A statement of what kind of work you want to do

- A positioning statement: Your professional identity, key competencies and unique strengths (differentiating you from other candidates in the same profession)

- Supporting material:
    - Accomplishment stories (highlighting your skills)
    - Exit statement and responses (preferably proactive) to predictable questions

Questions to Explore

- *Is my resume an effective marketing piece? Does it fit me as an individual and speak to my value?*

- *Do my positioning statement and resume support my professional objective?*

- *Are they appropriate to the organizations and industries I plan to target?*

- *What does a hiring manager need to know about me to make an informed decision?*

- *Do my communications tools deliver this message clearly?*

- *What will differentiate me from other candidates? Does my communications strategy reflect it?*

- *What am I likely to be asked in an interview? What accomplishment stories will I tell to illustrate my capabilities?*

Suggested Actions

- **Review and be prepared to discuss the skills, interests and experiences you identified while defining your professional objective.** Select the ones you believe a hiring manager would most likely want in a candidate for the type of work you are seeking.
- **Define your unique advantage in the marketplace.** Be clear about what differentiates you from (and makes you more attractive than) the average candidate for the job you want.
- **Discuss your overall communications strategy with one objective person or more,** preferably people who know the companies and positions you will be targeting.
- **Create a series of communications tools that all express the same themes or core ideas:**

  1. **Exit statement.** Write a careful statement that explains why you are in the market for a new position, and practice it out loud.
  2. **Positioning statement.** Craft a brief statement that conveys your professional objective, key qualifications and uniqueness for use in conversations. Practice it out loud.
  3. **Resume.** Create a resume that conveys your professional objective and qualifications effectively to your target market. Have a career consultant review it or ask for feedback from colleagues.
  4. **Accomplishment stories.** Write and practice telling stories that illustrate how you have made a difference in your other assignments.
  5. **References.** Prepare a list of professional references.

Preparing Your Exit Statement

Your exit statement answers the question: *Why are you looking for a new job?* You can think of it as your press release because it is the device that tells the world about your transition. An effective exit statement is brief, non-defensive and positive. When applicable, it lets others know that your departure was not due to any fault of yours.

SAMPLE Exit Statements

- *As a result of the merger of Walnut Industries and Parsons Products, 300 positions were eliminated, including mine. I am now exploring opportunities that will take full advantage of my extensive management experience, as well as my engineering and manufacturing background, in the food and chemical industries.*

- *The recent reorganization of Technical Publishing has afforded me the opportunity to explore new options. With my record of improving profits, extending market penetration, developing new products and managing significant cost containment, my objective is to locate a position as Senior Operating Executive in an international publishing environment.*

- *The recent acquisition of Larchwood Enterprises by Tangent Corporation created a number of duplicate functions and positions. Because of these duplications, a number of positions have been eliminated, including mine. I look forward to joining the management team of a new venture in electronics. I know that many of them will value my 15 years of experience in successfully turning around struggling companies.*

Your Exit Statement

Use the space below to draft your exit statement. Be sure to check it with two or three objective people before finalizing it.

_____

_____

_____

_____

_____

_____

Composing Your Positioning Statement

Your positioning statement is a fundamental communications tool you will use in conversations throughout your search in networking meetings and interviews. You also will use written versions of it in your cover letters and on your resume where it becomes the basis for your summary statement.

Your positioning statement responds to a request that you are likely to hear quite frequently during your conversations with people: Tell me about yourself. It actually presents you with a great opportunity to succinctly and positively position yourself in the minds of listeners. After you have written your statement, practice it out loud so that it comes out naturally and unrehearsed.

Guidelines for Composing Your Positioning Statement

Challenge yourself to keep your position statement concise – under two minutes. Structure it around the following four general categories:

1. **Profession.** Begin by stating your professional identity in the present tense (I am an information systems manager). Create a vivid personal image by associating yourself with your true profession and/or professional level (rather than your previous job title or organization). While your job title is vice president, you might consider marketing executive a more accurate portrait.

2. **Expertise.** When expressing your expertise, focus on the competencies and skills you identified in Milestone 2. For example, a human resources manager might discuss competencies in employee relations, training and development and benefits administration. An information systems manager might claim competencies in identifying and defining business problems, developing solutions through creative reengineering and maximizing profitability through the strategic application of technology.

3. **Types of Organizations/Environments.** Summarize the environments or organizations in which you have worked, such as a Fortune 100 firm, large insurance company, small consulting firm, entrepreneurial business, government agency or nonprofit entity. You may mention other types of activities, such as teaching, participating on the board of a business or a nonprofit organization or taking a leadership role in a professional association.

4. **Unique Strengths.** Articulate the qualities that differentiate you from others in your field, emphasizing a particularly deep (and marketable) technical knowledge, an exceptional approach to problem solving, or some other specialty or focus that sets you apart.

Positioning Statements

Note in the following examples that, while each person uses different methods to introduce strengths and expertise, each manages to create a clear impression of value to potential employers.

> **SAMPLE** ## Positioning Statements
>
> - *I am an information systems specialist focusing on the application of technology to business functions in the areas of marketing, sales, manufacturing, logistics and accounting. My field of experience is diverse. I have worked with a Fortune 500 firm as well as a small entrepreneurial business. I am now serving as an adjunct professor at Oxbridge College. My strengths include data administration, strategic planning, data warehousing, and relational database design, development and implementation.*
>
> - *I am a senior corporate officer with extensive expertise in operational responsibilities, including P&L, strategic planning and financial management. I have been particularly effective in increasing profitability, growing revenues and managing costs. My organization showed solid incremental gains in market share and still maintained operational efficiencies. One of my strengths is building management teams that value cross-functional working relationships.*

Your Positioning Statement

Use the space below to draft your own positioning statement.

_____

_____

_____

_____

_____

_____

_____

_____

Constructing Your Resume

Your resume is often the first impression a future employer has of you. As one of your key sales tools, it presents an overview of what you have done in the past and implies what you can do for a potential employer in the future.

THE PURPOSES OF A RESUME:

- **A sales brochure**

  You are the product your resume is selling. It can be used as a direct mail piece or a point-of-sale aid. Regardless of how you use it, the primary purpose of a resume is to sell you to your target market. As one of your key sales tools, your resume should stress the benefits derived by others who have used your services. Keep your target market in mind when writing it. Highlight the end results of your activities: what you accomplished.

- **A calling card**

  Your resume is an overview. It cannot and should not tell everything about you. Rather, it is a brief summary of what you have done in the past and implies what you can do in the future. It should be short (no more than two pages) and easy to read. Make this first impression a true representation of you: direct, effective and professional.

- **A reminder**

  After an interview an impression of you remains. The resume supports that personal impression and helps the interviewer remember you. Therefore, it should present a clear picture of you, the job candidate. Review your resume with this in mind. Be sure it is neat, well laid out, consistent and stresses what you have accomplished, as well as your areas of expertise.

- **A way to direct the interview**

  The way you structure your resume can help direct the interviewer's attention to specific accomplishments and relevant experiences. Review your resume to be sure they are easily visible.

 Tips and Techniques

Handling Special Situations

Single employer

If you have had only one employer but have had a series of job titles within that organization, highlight the years within each position and eliminate the total number of years with the company. You can show a potential employer that you can adapt to change by emphasizing new skills and responsibilities.

Many short-term positions

If you have had many short-term employers and many positions with those employers, emphasize only the dates with each employer (not the position). This will give the impression of more stable employment.

Self-employment

If you were self-employed, you may wish to give yourself an appropriate job title, e.g., consultant or vice president sales and marketing. Titles like owner or self-employed do not convey what you actually did.

Unpaid assignments

If you have had an internship or have done volunteer work relevant to your targeted career path, it is not necessary to include a notation that it was unpaid work. Keep in mind that your resume is a statement of the capabilities, skills, expertise and benefits you can bring to your future employer.

Ten Parts of a Resume

All resumes should contain certain vital information. While the Professional Objective is listed here, you may prefer to omit that part and just let your Summary Statement follow the Heading.

1. **Heading**
   List your name, address, telephone number(s) and email address. If you use an answering machine or a service, be sure the message is professional, and check your messages regularly.

2. **Professional Objective** (optional)
   Having a professional objective – a concise statement of what you want to do – helps you keep your resume consistent and focused. It is your option as to whether or not you include an objective on your resume. If you do, it can serve as an advertising headline, telling what services you have to offer. If it is not included, most readers will assume that you are seeking work similar to your most recent position.

3. **Summary Statement**
   Write a concise statement summarizing experience, areas of expertise, technical or professional skills, traits and any distinctions. The summary emphasizes key information detailed in the body of the resume. Since it includes the strongest arguments for hiring you, use key words that match what your target market desires.

4. **Employment History**
   Company names, years employed and job titles should be included.

5. **Responsibilities Statements**
   Summarize information selected from your job description, special assignments and general duties that a potential employer might find of interest. One paragraph for each recent job listed and one sentence for earlier jobs is adequate.

6. **Accomplishment Statements**
   These statements should show your achievements and contributions to an organization – three to six for your most recent job, one to three for prior jobs. Think about different performance measurements important to your profession. Omit them for very old jobs.

7. **Education**
   Summarize your educational background in reverse chronological order, including your highest degree and university. You may include the date and more details if you have graduated within the past five years. Omit if your education is not one of your assets.

8. **Professional Development and Training**
   List additional training or courses that support and are relevant to your job objective. This section can be separate or included as part of your education with the heading: Education/Training and Development.

9. **Memberships**
   Include memberships and offices held in professional associations, boards and community activities that support your objective.

10. **Other Categories**
    If relevant to your objective, list languages, licenses, certifications, military experience, technical skills and the titles of publications you have written.

Guidelines for Constructing Your Resume

There are no hard and fast rules for designing and constructing a resume. However, these guidelines will assist you in organizing your thoughts and writing an understandable and convincing resume. The following guidelines basically apply to both hard copy and electronic resumes. Consider these four categories:

1. Overall

- **Your professional objective indicates the functional area in which you want to work.** If you include a professional objective on your resume, be sure that everything in your resume supports it and nothing contradicts it.

- **Keep your target market in mind.** Ask yourself: If I were the employer, would I interview this person? Unless the answer is an unqualified yes, you still have some work to do.

- **Proofread the final product for correct spelling, punctuation, grammar and typographical errors.** Have an independent, detail-minded person proofread it for errors you might have missed.

- **Start with a first draft.** Begin the process with the knowledge that a topnotch resume rarely is written the first time. Expect to do several revisions.

2. Content

- **Describe specific responsibilities and highlight accomplishments using positive language to describe results.**

- **Support all activities and accomplishments with specific results and benefits;** qualify or quantify your accomplishments wherever possible.

- **Summarize early employment by briefly describing your function.** All content must support your professional objective and sell you to your prospective employer.

- **Highlight your work history selectively,** specifically drawing attention to what the market is buying. There may be a good reason to spend 50% of your description on something that occupied only 25% of your time.

- **Do not include anything that will raise doubts or cause you to be screened out.** Deal with such information in an interview, not in a resume.

- **Do not list references.** Reserve them for the interview. Do not use the phrase: References available upon request.

- **Do not overemphasize your educational background.** If you have been out of school five years or more, you are selling your work experience rather than your academic record.

- **Do not leave any gaps between employment dates.** List jobs by year rather than by month and year. If a gap occurred, list the time with a brief explanation, i.e., "Sabbatical 2010-2011."

- **Do not include extraneous or personal information that does not support your objective,** such as age, marital status or number of children.

- **Do not exaggerate or misrepresent your experience.**

- **Do not include a snapshot of yourself.**

3. Style

- **Avoid using "I" in your statements;** instead, begin sentences or phrases with action words.

- **Use the present tense to describe your current or most recent job.** However, if describing something already implemented or achieved, use the past tense. All previous positions should be described in the past tense.

- **Write out all numbers up to and including the number nine.** Use numerals for 10 to 999,999 (except at the beginning of a sentence).

- **Use a direct, active writing style.** Use short phrases rather than complete sentences. If you can say something in three words, do not use 10. Keep paragraphs under six lines.

- **Use key words and phrases appropriate to your next, not your previous, employer or industry.** Hiring managers and recruiters will review resumes looking for key words that match the company's and the job's needs.

- **Do not use abbreviations** (e.g., HR for human resources). Use professional or technical jargon only if it is relevant to the position and you are sure all readers will understand it.

- **Use capital letters, dashes, underlining or bullets (•) to emphasize certain items** and make them stand out on your hard copy resume. Use these symbols judiciously or they lose their effect.

4. Format and Layout

- **Keep the resume to one or two pages.** Employers and recruiters simply do not have the time to read a lengthy document. If you use a second page, be sure it is longer than a couple of paragraphs.

- **Include your name, phone number and a page number on your second page** in case the pages become separated.

- **Make sure all of your key selling points appear on the first page if your resume is two pages.** If a key point is best said on page two, include it in the summary statement on page one.

- **Make your resume visually appealing and easy to read and scan.** Use lots of white space and wide margins.

- **Do not use odd-sized paper, overly fancy stock, color, style, font** or anything considered eccentric or difficult to fax or scan.

- **Select headlines and initial phrases that support your main message.**

- **Pick a resume format and be consistent.**

- **Lay out your resume so that a job description or a sentence on the first page does not run over to the second.**

- **Be aware of information or dates that could be used to screen you out of consideration.**

- **Devote more space to recent jobs than to earlier ones.** Employers generally are interested in your most recent experience.

- **Reverse chronological order is standard for listing employers.** Include the geographic location next to the employer's name.

Resume Formats

The two most common resume formats are the chronological and the functional.
Sometimes a combination of the two is used.

The Chronological Resume

The chronological resume is the most frequently used – and accepted – resume format.

It lists work experience in reverse chronological order, outlining your job history from the most recent job backwards, with greater emphasis on the most recent job. It provides clear information on job titles, areas of responsibility and periods of employment for each employer, and accomplishments are clearly tied to companies and time frames.

The chronological resume is helpful when...
- Your career history shows growth and development.
- Your job objective is similar to your recent experience.
- Your previous employers have been prestigious.
- You are applying for a position in highly traditional fields or organizations.

The chronological resume is <u>not</u> helpful when...
- Your objective is very different from your experience (i.e., changing careers).
- Your work history is spotty.
- You have been absent from the job market.
- You have changed employers frequently.

The Functional Resume

The functional resume format is designed to stress the qualifications of the job seeker, with less emphasis on specific employers and dates.

Some functional formats found in popular books on resumes do not include a work history. However, the format presented here does include a work history because omitting it nearly always raises questions in the reader's mind.

The functional format is particularly suitable for job seekers who want to make a significant change in their field or functional areas. However, the decision to use a functional resume should be carefully weighed because many employers are suspicious of them and prefer chronological resumes.

The functional resume is helpful when:
- Your objective is very different from your experience.
- You want to emphasize skills/abilities not used in recent work experience.
- Your experience has been gained in different, relatively unconnected jobs.
- You are entering the job market after an absence.

The functional resume is <u>not</u> helpful when:
- Your past employers have been prestigious.
- You want to focus attention on the pattern of your career growth.
- You are applying for a position in a highly traditional field.

Writing Your Summary Statement

The purpose of the summary statement on a resume is to encapsulate the experience, areas of expertise, technical or professional skills and traits detailed in the body of your resume. Since it includes the strongest arguments for hiring you, use key words that match what your target market desires and/or highlight your key attributes.

Five Samples of Summary Statements

SUMMARY

Senior Marketing Executive experienced with diverse technologies. Innovative strategist with proven ability to identify, launch and manage products and services in both emerging and established markets. Demonstrated competence in start-ups and Fortune 500 organizations.

- Profitable P&L experience
- Public and private offerings
- Distribution and support
- Mergers, joint ventures

CUSTOMER SERVICE LEADER

Over 10 years of experience managing customer service personnel. Strengths include implementation and maintenance of a state-of-the-art customer service organization. Successful in resolving customers' concerns in both corporate and field environments.

SUMMARY

Results-oriented Controller with both hands-on and management experience in all aspects of finance and accounting. Strategic member of an executive team that built a national business through mergers and acquisitions. Effective in creating a positive and productive work environment.

- Business planning and financial analysis
- Systems development and integration
- Growth forecasting
- HRIS

SENIOR OPERATING EXECUTIVE

Proven track record in increasing earnings in diverse markets and industries. Proficient in turning around organizations and balancing shareholder, customer and employee needs. Developed strong teams by providing support, making expectations clear and treating others fairly and with dignity. Respected by a wide range of functional groups from craft workers to board members.

SUMMARY

Sales management professional with a successful track record of developing and implementing strategies and programs that resulted in opening new market segments to sell value-added products. Visionary with ability to project market needs, develop new products to improve profits, increase sales and extend market penetration.

Creating Your Accomplishment Statements

Your accomplishment statements have their roots in the accomplishment stories you did in Milestone 2. In that exercise, you developed stories describing a situation you faced, the obstacles you faced, the actions you took and the results you achieved (SOAR). Your accomplishment statements briefly capture the actions you took and the results you achieved. Make each statement interesting, but keep some intrigue as to how you achieved the accomplishment. After all, you want to be called in for an interview.

Samples of Accomplishment Statements

QUANTITY

- Developed a sales strategy that directly increased customer base by 20%.

- Redesigned the production line, increasing daily output by 2,000 units.

- Developed a training program that contributed to a 35% reduction in errors.

- Entered 15 new markets, increasing market share.

- Developed a safety program that reduced accident fines by 15%.

QUALITY

- Successfully conducted a presentation for key project stakeholders. Unsolicited feedback was overwhelmingly positive.

- Designed a new training program that resulted in an improvement in evaluations from 3.2 to 4.8 on a 5-point scale.

- Implemented a new employee benefit program. More than 90% of the employees identified the changes as improvements.

- Hired a new printing firm that improved quality of the marketing materials.

- Designed a user-friendly operations manual that is currently being used by employees.

- Reorganized a tracking system that improved document retrieval.

- Made product design changes resulting in fewer rejects.

PRODUCTIVITY

- Automated a claim processing system that reduced the turnaround time from two weeks to two days.

- Implemented a new phone system that reduced average answering speed from eight minutes to less than one minute.

- Completed the project ahead of schedule.

- Developed and introduced a unique product that was the first in the marketplace.

COST / REVENUE

- Negotiated a contract that saved the department over $500,000.

- Reduced overhead by 30%.

- Developed a new product that increased quarterly revenue by $50,000.

- Turned a troubled operation around from a negative $238,000 to a positive $1,570,000.

- Increased sales over 40%.

On the following page is a list of effective sentence openers to help you create your statements.

Effective Sentence Openers for Accomplishment Statements

absorbed	dealt with	identified	observed	selected
achieved	decided	illustrated	obtained	served
acted	defined	implemented	opened	serviced
added	delivered	improved	operated	set up
administered	demonstrated	improvised	organized	shipped
advised	designed	increased	outlined	showed
analyzed	determined	influenced	overhauled	simplified
applied	developed	informed	oversaw	sold
appraised	diagnosed	initiated		solved
approved	directed	innovated	packed	sorted
arranged	discovered	inspected	patrolled	staffed
assembled	distributed	installed	persuaded	standardized
assisted	diverted	instituted	photocopied	started
attended	duplicated	instructed	picked out	strengthened
automated		integrated	planned	studied
	edited	interpreted	positioned	supervised
balanced	encouraged	interviewed	posted	supplied
bought	enlisted	introduced	prepared	supported
budgeted	ensured	invented		systematized
built	equipped	invested	qualified	
	established	investigated	questioned	tabulated
carried	evaluated			tailored
centralized	expanded	judged	raised	taught
changed	expedited		read	tended
checked	experimented	launched	realized	totaled
clarified	extracted	learned	received	tracked
cleaned		lectured	recognized	trained
coached	facilitated	led	recorded	transacted
collaborated	fed	leveraged	recruited	transferred
collated	finalized	liquidated	reduced	translated
compared	financed	listed	refined	transported
compiled	folded	located	related	treated
completed	fostered	logged	reorganized	
composed	found	lowered	reported	uncovered
computed	founded		represented	undertook
conceived	furnished	maintained	researched	unified
condensed		managed	responded	updated
controlled	generated	measured	restored	upgraded
converted	governed	merged	restricted	utilized
conveyed	guaranteed	minimized	retrieved	
coordinated	guided	modernized	revamped	verbalized
corrected		modified	reviewed	verified
corresponded	handled	motivated	revised	
counseled	headed			weighed
created	helped	negotiated		withstood
	hired	notified		worked
	hypothesized	numbered		wrote

Chronological Resume

NAME
Address
City / State / Zip Code

Telephone Number   **Email Address**

SUMMARY

A Human Resources executive with experience as a strategic member of corporate leadership teams. Strong business background developed through line and staff positions in various industries. A visionary with the ability to serve as a catalyst for profitable and orderly workforce change. Able to establish rapport and credibility with diverse groups ranging from union members to board members. Solution-oriented with an eye toward bottom-line results.

- Mergers and Acquisitions
- RIF/Reorganization
- Profit Centers
- Executive/Board Compensation

PROFESSIONAL EXPERIENCE

SANTINI FOODS, Chicago, IL   **2012-Present**
Vice President, Human Resources
Run a human resource profit center for the food business line of this global $20 billion consumer packaged goods company.

- Provided strategic counsel during mergers and acquisitions regarding culture integration and human resource cost benefit analysis that were critical factors in purchase decisions.
- Led the company through a comprehensive reengineering, work redesign and process improvement effort that resulted in cost savings and improved quality and efficiencies.
- Negotiated compensation and benefits package during union negotiations on time (for the first time in 12 years), with net savings of $12 million over a five-year period.
- Outsourced several functions. Decreased the human resource budget by 30%, while increasing productivity, efficiencies and quality.
- Developed a new Human Resource Information System, created a human resource service center and implemented a payroll conversion that improved timeliness and compliance.

YUMMY GUMMIES, Chicago, IL   **2008-2012**
Director, Human Resources
Directed all human resources for 10 customer groups for this global $2 billion candy manufacturer.

- Championed a corporate culture change from bureaucratic and entitlement to participative.
- Initiated the creation of the executive succession plan, utilizing a 360-degree feedback instrument for executive development, which increased corporate bench strength.
- Fashioned a bonus that increased production by 200% without sacrificing quality.

Page 1 of 2

SAMPLE

NAME	Telephone Number

Manager, Human Resources   2004-2008

Provided all human resource functions for three customer groups.

- Applied Total Quality Management, Demand Flow Manufacturing and ISO 9000 to human resource operations resulting in streamlining, efficiencies and improved customer service.
- Directed the design and management of competency-based and skill-based compensation plans utilizing pay-at-risk, gain sharing and individual/team incentives.
- Reduced workers' compensation costs by 72%, from $180,000 to $50,400 during the first year and achieved Workers' Compensation Premium Certification.

SPARKLING BOTTLERS, Rolling Meadows, IL   1998-2004
Employment and Compensation Manager

Coordinated and managed the development and implementation of recruiting, employment and compensation programs for this $1.5 billion bottling plant.

- Increased employee retention by 20% and reduced associated costs of hiring.
- Designed, implemented and managed competitive compensation programs including employee incentive plans, which improved productivity and morale.

EDUCATION

Executive Development Program, J. L. Kellogg Graduate School of Management, Evanston, IL
BA, International Studies, Northwestern University, Evanston, IL
The Leadership Development Program, Center for Creative Leadership, Greensboro, NC

Numerous human resource and management programs, conferences and seminars, e.g., human resource shared services, strategic planning, organizational development, change management, mediation/ negotiation and employment law.

PROFESSIONAL CERTIFICATIONS

Senior Professional Human Resources (SPHR), Society of Human Resource Management
Certified Compensation Professional (CCP)

AFFILIATIONS

American Compensation Association
Society of Human Resource Management
American Society for Training and Development

Guidelines for Preparing Electronic Resumes

Both the paper, or hard copy, as well as the electronic resume may be needed in your job search activities. Be prepared to use both. Consider these additional guidelines for electronic resumes:

1. Overall	2. Style	3. Format and Layout
The Internet presents substantial networking as well as global job search opportunities. There are numerous sites on the Internet where you can search for job openings and apply online, post your resume, join news group discussions (bulletin boards by topic) and subscribe to job mailing lists (a job email notification system). It is important to keep in mind that the Internet is a public communication medium. Once you submit your resume, you lose control over who views it. Identifying and using sites you trust is advisable.	**Because hiring managers may receive literally thousands of electronic resumes** in response to a single job posting, it is important that your resume stands out. • **Use key words that match the needs typically requested in your field.** If marketing positions frequently mention e-commerce, use that language in your resume, e.g., "developed a global e-commerce system." • **If your job title was unique to your former employer,** explain it in more common language in parentheses next to the title, e.g., Service Excellence Coordinator (Quality Improvement Manager). • **Be succinct.** Use a strong summary statement and put your most important accomplishments up front. • **Adjust your page margins to one inch on top, bottom and left.** Adjust to two inches on the right. Change the justification to left alignment. Select a simple font, such as Times or Courier New, with the standard size of 12 points.	**While most Internet job postings today accept resumes in Microsoft Word,** some still require that you fill out a form and cut and paste a resume into a text box. The sizes of the text boxes can vary widely in width and result in the loss of your formatting because your text is wrapped down into the next line to fit the particular text box. Others will request an attachment, although that is usually less desirable because they can clutter up hard drives, may carry viruses, are not supported by all email programs and take time to download and access. Always be sure to follow the instructions provided on the preferred way to send your document electronically. Create a separate electronic version of your resume in an ASCII or text file. With your document open, save it with a new name and change the type of document to "text."

Use Special Resume When Changing Careers

If you intend to stay in your same industry and function, you are likely to have the quickest transition. The further you move away from your experience, the longer your transition could take. However, some people regard career transition as an ideal time to investigate changing careers and look into other industries or functions.

One effective way to make a career change is to identify other industries or functions that use the same skills and knowledge you used in your previous career. For example, a person coming out of insurance operations management will have had some sales or marketing responsibilities. If this person is interested in going into sales and moving from a mature industry to a growth industry, a change to selling software to insurance companies would be an easier transition than Internet sales.

As we explained earlier in this chapter, a functional resume is particularly helpful for people who are changing careers. To create a functional resume for career change, identify the skills your new target industry or function values. You can do this by reading the ads and researching trends.

After you have done your research and identified your relevant skills and accomplishments, re-read your chronological resume and move your accomplishment statements under the appropriate categories. Delete examples that do not fit and, if necessary, add additional accomplishments from experience not on your chronological resume. Make sure you use language that is more generic and less industry specific. For example, a person coming out of the insurance industry would want to use "customers" instead of "insureds."

On the following pages are examples of a chronological and a functional resume for the same person. The functional resume sample was written to help the person make a transition from banking to a corporate finance role.

SAMPLE **Chronological Resume**

NAME
Address
City / State / Zip Code

Telephone Number   **Email Address**

SUMMARY

A senior banker with experience in all aspects of commercial banking, compliance, branch banking, asset management and special asset liquidation. Effective in starting up branches, establishing a market presence and winning customers from the competition. Experienced in turning poor performing operations into profitable centers. Education at the Graduate School of Banking and Finance, Madison, Wisconsin.

EXPERIENCE

GOTHAM BANK, New York, NY   **2012 - Present**
Senior Vice President

Chief operating officer for a turnaround $60 million asset branch and a $20 million asset start-up. Manage staff in excess of 55 employees with a $5 million budget.

- Increased asset base from $17 million to $53 million, with a profit increase from a negative $235,000 to a positive $2,750,000, representing a 4% return on assets within two years.
- Instrumental in improving Uniform Composite Rating from a level 2 to a level 1 in one year.
- Resolved credit extension problems. Set up policies and procedures that insured regulatory compliance and standardization of reporting to federal and state agencies.
- Negotiated a medical services program for the major community hospitals to provide financial support for the hospitals' physician recruiting programs.
- As Senior V.P. for start-up operations in Edison, NJ, was instrumental in accomplishing a deposit base of $15,000,000 and a loan base of $18,000,000 in a 16-month period.

BJ INVESTMENTS, Paterson, NJ   **2003 - 2012**
CEO

Consultant to the banking and communications industries on funding, compliance and technology transaction issues.

- Created long-term strategies for businesses. Developed and implemented policies and procedures that improved market standing. Successfully led corporate headquarters expansions.
- Developed a strategy for aggressive lending programs and the installation of a data processing center serving over six commercial banks that transformed P&L into profitability.
- Developed an expense reduction strategy for a telecommunications reseller of AT&T, MCI and Sprint products. Supervised billing and collection programs and software that facilitated timely wire transfer of revenues from principals.

NAME	Telephone Number

- Automated in-house systems for employers and clients, increasing cash flow by 30%.
- Secured funding for Continental Service Corporation's capital acquisition that resulted in a multimillion-dollar collection service entity to the title insurance industry.

FIRST AMERICAN BANK, Newark, NJ   **2000 - 2003**
Executive Vice President and Chief Administrative Officer

Developed corporate standards, policies and procedures for 30 branches. Served as Compliance/Community Reinvestment Act Officer.

- Developed banks that had fallen into disfavor with the Comptroller of the Currency into ones that surpassed regulatory requirements.
- Negotiated compensation and benefits packages for officers, employees and the board.

ADDITIONAL RELEVANT EXPERIENCE
Executive Vice President and CEO of First Security Bank, N.A., Paramus, NJ
Vice President at First National Bank, Pleasantville, NY

EDUCATION AND TRAINING
Graduate School of Banking and Finance, Graduate Certificate, Madison, WI
BS, Business, State University of New York, Binghamton, NY

LICENSES
National Association of Security Dealers, NASD License, New York, NY

AFFILIATIONS
American Bankers Association
America's Community Bankers
Electronic Banking Association
Independent Bankers Association
Chamber of Commerce, New York, NY

Page 2 of 2

SAMPLE Career Change Functional Resume

NAME
Address
City / State / Zip Code

Telephone Number   **Email Address**

OBJECTIVE: A corporate finance leadership position in an aggressive organization that values innovative solutions to further the success and profitability of business owners and clients.

SUMMARY

A senior executive and private consultant experienced in securing funding for corporate expansions, mergers and acquisitions and start-ups. Education at the Graduate School of Banking and Finance, Madison, Wisconsin with application in compliance, asset acquisition and management, and special asset liquidation.

PROVEN ABILITIES AND RESULTS

Business Funding and Growth Strategies

- Acquired capitalization for one of the first national disaster recovery facilities.
- Developed a marketing strategy for a telecommunications reseller. Supervised billing and collection programs and software that facilitated timely wire transfer of revenues.
- Secured funding for Continental Service Corporation's capital acquisition that resulted in a multimillion-dollar collection service entity to the title insurance industry.
- Created long-term strategies for businesses. Developed and implemented policies and procedures that improved market standing.

Profitability

- Developed banks that had fallen into disfavor with the Comptroller of the Currency into ones that surpassed regulatory requirements.
- Managed start-up operations in Edison, NJ; instrumental in accomplishing a deposit base of $15,000,000 and a loan base of $18,000,000 in a 16-month period.
- Developed a successful strategy for aggressive lending programs and the installation of a data processing center serving over six commercial banks that increased revenue.

Credit and Operations Administration

- Instrumental in improving the Uniform Composite Rating of a state-chartered bank from a level 2 to a level 1 in a one-year period.
- Experienced in all aspects of commercial banking: administration, operations, loans, asset management, investments and capital acquisition. Led staff in excess of 55 employees; managed a budget in excess of $5 million and negotiated compensation and benefits packages for officers, employees and the board.

SAMPLE

NAME	Telephone Number

Problem Solving/Analysis
- Resolved credit extension problems. Set up policies and procedures that ensured regulatory compliance and standardization of reporting to federal and state agencies.
- Developed and administered new programs, policies and procedures that reinstated the credibility and strength in the loan portfolios of several financially impaired banks.

Negotiating
- Secured a deal for a $15 million housing project between Union Pacific Railroad, Allied Chemical Corporation and First Security Bank.
- Negotiated a medical services program for the major community hospitals to provide financial support for the hospitals' physician recruiting programs.

Technology Application
- Automated in-house systems for employers and clients resulting in efficiencies.
- Developed an in-house data processing center for a commercial bank.

EXPERIENCE
Gotham Bank, New York, NY, Senior Vice President 2012-Present
BJ Investments, Paterson, NJ; CEO 2003-2012
First American Bank, Newark, NJ, EVP and Chief Administrative Officer 2000-2003

ADDITIONAL RELEVANT EXPERIENCE
Executive Vice President and CEO, First Security Bank, N.A., Paramus, NJ
Vice President, First National Bank, Pleasantville, NY

EDUCATION AND TRAINING
Graduate School of Banking and Finance, Graduate Certificate, Madison, WI
BS, Business, State University of New York, Binghamton, NY

LICENSE
National Association of Security Dealers, NASD License, New York, NY

AFFILIATIONS
American Bankers Association
Independent Bankers Association
Chamber of Commerce, New York, NY

Using Email in Job Search

Email is fast and convenient. It can be used to respond to job openings and to keep in touch with your contacts. Even though it appears to be an informal way of communicating, the same rules that apply to composing letters apply to writing email messages: they should be formal, polite and make a good impression. Here are some guidelines:

- **If you use email in your job search, be sure your email address is appropriate for the world of business** – ralphyboy@example.net may not be consistent with the image you wish to project to a potential employer. If necessary, open a separate email account for this purpose. There are a number of free services. For the purposes of job search, using your name (such as john.smith@ example.net) will be seen as more professional and increase your name recognition.

- **If you have any doubts as to whether email is the appropriate medium, send a letter by mail.** For instance, sending a thank you note by email to a contact after a meeting is fine. However, a follow-up letter following a formal interview might be better handled by regular mail – unless the interviewer has provided an email address and specifically suggested it as a way to stay in touch.

- **Use the subject line to your advantage.** Include either the job opening or summarize your experience in the title.

- **Spell-check your document and double-check grammar.** Limit words with all upper case letters – their use is considered "shouting."

- **Avoid common email abbreviations** such as TTYL (talk to you later) or BTW (by the way) unless they are also commonly used in everyday English, such as FYI. The same is true for email cues, such as smiling faces.

- **Personalize your message to the recipient.** When sending a message to someone you do not know, it is safest to use the same salutation as you would in a letter ("Dear Ms. Jones") and close with "Sincerely" or "Best regards." Failure to put a person's name makes the email seem cold.

- **Include your email address, street address and phone number** after your name in the closing so that they are all easy to find.

- **As with resumes, use plain text** and avoid fancy fonts, colors and lines.

Writing Cover Letters

Unless you personally hand a resume to a prospective employer, a cover letter usually accompanies it. Every cover letter follows a general formula that can be adapted to the specific need. Remember: Always thank the employer for time and consideration. Here's the format:

Date

Address

Salutation

> **Paragraph one:** Explain why you are writing in a way that arouses interest. Display your knowledge of the reader's company or group.

In response to your advertisement in the *Wall Street Journal* for a Vice President of Field Sales, I am enclosing my resume. I have been watching the growth of Superior with great interest over the past year, particularly the creation of high-powered sales teams as a way of increasing your sales volume and profitability.

> **Paragraph two:** Briefly describe your qualifications and accomplishments and identify the relevant job title.

Most recently, as Vice President, Field Sales, for Namebrand Pharmaceuticals, I managed $160 million in annual sales with nearly 100 direct sales people and 16 brokers across two-thirds of the United States. I worked for Namebrand for seven years in a number of capacities under five separate corporate umbrellas.

> **Paragraph three:** Answer the question: Why should I hire you? Relate yourself to the company or group. (This paragraph may be omitted if you prefer a shorter letter.)

Namebrand and Superior have built reputations as hard-driving, profit-oriented organizations. Having proven myself in one of the most tough-minded companies by taking an entrepreneurial approach to account, personnel and sales management, I would like to bring my talents to your company, a company that rewards creative drive, solid execution and hard work.

> **Paragraph four:** Take the initiative, request action, ask for an interview, suggest a time to meet and tell the employer when you will call.

I look forward to meeting with you to discuss in more detail how my background and qualifications can work for you. I appreciate your consideration and will call you next week to see when we might meet.

Sincerely,

Name

Encl: resume

Compiling Your Reference List

List your references on a separate sheet of paper, not on your resume. With your professional objective in mind, provide a concise, targeted list of people who can give an overall view of your abilities and talk about your skills. Reference checking is usually done by telephone, most often in the final stage of hiring. Some employers check references only after hiring; some do not check at all.

Guidelines for Compiling Your Reference List

- **Use a multilayered approach to the list:** people whom you have worked for, people who have worked for you and colleagues with whom you have worked. Former bosses are a great reference. If you leave your former or current boss off your list, be prepared to explain why. Do not say anything if you are not asked.

- **Include people you have worked with** on task forces and team projects, vendors, suppliers and clients, where appropriate, and people in professional associations who are good personal contacts. If you have done volunteer work, include references from those projects.

- **Include your relationship to your references** in a very brief manner after their contact information.

Guidelines for Handling Your References

- **If your name has changed for any reason,** make sure your references know you by your new name.

- **Ask your references' permission** to use their names.

- **Send your references a copy of your resume and a cover letter.** These act as convenient tools to organize their thoughts and jog memories of your results and achievements.

- **Coach your references** on what skills to highlight when called.

- **Ask them to tell you** when they are called for a reference.

- **Consider all references** as networking **contacts and cultivate those relationships.**

- **Do not attach your reference** sheet to your resume – save it for the interview.

 Reference List

NAME
Address
City / State / Zip Code

Telephone Number   **Email Address**

REFERENCES

Mr. John B. Gillespie, CEO
Widget Soundbite Company, Portland, Oregon
Telephone Number
Email Address
(My manager at Widget Soundbite Company)

Mr. William T. Strayhorn
Vice President, Engineering
Protel Telecommunications, Renton, Washington
Telephone Number
Email Address
(My direct report at former employer, Systemic Energy Resources)

Ms. Cora Walton
Consultant
Anacortes, Washington
Telephone Number
Email Address
(Personal Referral)

Creating Your Online Profiles

Just as you spent all that time making your resume perfect, you need to devote time to crafting your online profiles. Simply inserting your name and some basic information is not the formula for success.

While you're researching companies you want to work for, employers and recruiters are researching you, too. Most corporate recruiters and hiring managers are realizing the power of social media and are turning to websites to source and screen candidates.

Sometimes employers even seek out candidates after seeing their profiles on LinkedIn – even before the candidate makes contact. So the value of an exceptional online profile is obvious. How you present yourself online could have a significant impact on your career.

Not being represented online in today's technological world, in fact, could have a negative effect.

Your online profile needs to reflect the information on your resume. And it needs to be done in the same professional manner. Your virtual world image is very important.

LinkedIn is a Must

One of your first tasks in job search should be to create a profile on LinkedIn, the professional social media site that hiring managers utilize the most. This is a must for those in job search. Even after you're employed, you need to keep it updated so others can seek you out.

Facebook, Twitter and Beyond

Although considered more a site of a personal nature, Facebook's power and broad reach with 600 million registered users is undeniable.

The number of employers using the site to find out more about their potential hires also is on the rise. Facebook is a good way for companies to find out if a potential employee is a good fit for the company. Facebook also is trying to make the professional connections easier through its app Branchout.

Twitter, the microblogging site, is the other one of the big three social media sites. Building relationships and making contacts via this method will take time. The important thing is to keep your profile and tweets professional too. You never know what hiring manager may be looking.

Of course, thousands more social media sites exist and more emerge daily. Many of these sites are targeting the job search market. Don't get caught devoting all your job search time here. Use what works for you, but try to be represented where employers are looking most.

LinkedIn: Keep it Professional

LinkedIn is the largest professional networking tool online. For individuals in career transition, an updated LinkedIn profile is very important. This site is the single most important social networking tool for your career.

Your profile should be filled out completely, with your relevant work experience, specialties, skills, what you're looking for, and recommendations from former colleagues. Once you have established an impressive profile, you can use LinkedIn proactively to build your network, develop your expertise, find job leads and connect with recruiters and hiring managers at the companies of your choice.

SET UP YOUR PROFILE IN 8 STEPS:

1. **Sign up.** Go to LinkedIn.com. Fill out your name, email and the password of your choice.

2. **Fill out every major area of your profile.** Hiring managers will be looking. These include:
   - **Summary:** What is your personal brand your story that you want to tell employers?
   - **Specialties/Keywords:** What are your areas of expertise? Use keywords relevant to you experience – this will help optimize your profile to come up when recruiters are searching for candidates.
   - **Past Experience:** Put in all relevant past jobs. You don't have to list every job you have ever had, but certainly list the most recent as well as those jobs most relevant to the position you are seeking.

3. **Carefully word your headline.** This should tell your brand in one short sentence. For example, 'Experienced Communications Professional with Fortune 500 Experience'.

4. **Use a photo.** This will help with recognition when recruiters see you online. It also will help make your profile look more complete and professional. Make sure it's a professional looking headshot.

5. **Connect with friends and colleagues.** As LinkedIn is based on the strength of your network and connections, this is especially important. Upload your email contacts/address book. Find out who is a member of LinkedIn and invite them to connect. Make sure you add friends, family, former colleagues, professional contacts and acquaintances.

6. **Ask for recommendations.** Once you have connected with people on LinkedIn, ask individuals whom you particularly trust for a professional recommendation. If they write one, it will be displayed on your profile – and will be visible as a testament of your skill to potential employers.

7. **Join professional groups.** Many industries and professional associations have networking groups. Do a LinkedIn search for your field and join. Groups can help you keep up with your industry's news, to network and to find job leads.

8. **Check for 100 percent completeness.** When you are done, LinkedIn informs you how complete your profile is. If you're not hitting 100, then go back and revisit sections that might require a little more work.

Tips and Techniques

- **Write a personal note with each LinkedIn invitation.** When sending an invitation to connect on LinkedIn, the automatic default is the invitation text *"I'd like to add you to my professional network on LinkedIn."* This is the easy way, but we recommend you write a personal note. It will set you apart from the crowd.

- **Send an invitation to connect right after a meeting.** If you meet someone new at an event, for instance, and see them as a valuable contact, send a LinkedIn invitation within a day or two afterwards. This will ensure they remember meeting you.

- **Take action proactively.** Search for hiring managers and related key words. LinkedIn allows you to search based on keywords in other people's profiles, so take advantage of this feature to search for hiring managers and others who work at companies of interest.

Facebook: Respect Your Privacy

Facebook is the world's largest social networking site with more than 600 million registered users. And that number is growing with Facebook's ongoing integration into smart phones and Apple interfaces. That's a lot of networking potential that job seekers don't want to miss.

Since Facebook is traditionally a personal networking site where users share everything from their wild weekend in Bora Bora to their recipes, our best advice is USER BEWARE. Especially when you're in an active job search, you don't want a potential employer calling up your profile and seeing photos of that last wild party. Use discretion … and use the privacy settings.

SET UP YOUR PROFILE IN 6 STEPS:

1. **Sign up.** Go to Facebook.com. Fill out your name, email and the password of your choice. It will also ask for your sex and birthday, but it will be your option later if you want that revealed to the world. Perhaps you just want to put the month and the date of your birthday without revealing the year.

2. **Fill out the Bio/About Me section.** This is a great place to tell your story and share your personal brand. Write a few short sentences explaining what you're all about, what your background is, and what your interests are.

3. **Fill out the Work/Education section.** This basic information always is important to showcase.

4. **Fill out contact information.** Always make sure you can be reached.

5. **Consider other sections.** Posting the other personal items such as favorite sports, books or movies is totally up to you. Just beware of categories such a religious beliefs or political views – whereas employers are not supposed to discriminate on such matters, it does happen.

6. **Set your Privacy Controls.** If your site is even slightly questionable, this is the best way to avoid potential employers from counting you out. Facebook offers a wide range of privacy settings, which allow you to set your profile anywhere from totally public to totally private – and anything in between. Because employers will be searching for you, it is important to make sure that only professional content is publicly viewable to recruiters, and that all other personal content is made private and viewable only by your friends and family. The privacy settings can be accessed in the top navigation bar along with the account settings.

Twitter: Make it Short and Tweet

Where can you get instant information on your targeted companies and industries from insiders, industry professionals and recruiters? You can use Twitter, the free social networking micro-blogging service that allows users to send tweets of up to 140 characters to the Twitter website.

We caution job hunters not to devote an inordinate amount of time here, but it does have a top spot in the social networking world with 190 million users tweeting 65 million times a day. If you're in job search, following the feeds of tweeters related to targeted companies and industries can be useful. Twitter also is good for demonstrating thought leadership and interests by sharing links, articles and industry news, and engaging in conversations with other industry professionals.

SET UP YOUR PROFILE IN 5 STEPS:

1. **Sign up.** Go to Twitter.com. Fill out your name, username, password and an email address. Make sure you choose a username that is consistent with how you want people to recognize you online – such as your first and last name.

2. **Fill out your profile completely.** You never know if an employer is going to check out your profile after you have tweeted with an interesting industry article. Make sure you intrigue them – especially in the bio section.

3. **Add value in your tweets.** When you do devote time to Twitter, make sure it worthwhile. Don't talk about what you had for breakfast. Rather add something of value. Share articles you find interesting and links to your industry's news.

4. **Seek out interesting people to follow.** Use the "Find People" feature on Twitter to find suggested users in various industries. Check out the "Who to Follow" list of suggested users on the Twitter homepage. Actively engage anyone who could have a positive impact on your job search.

5. **Follow your industry Tweets.** Search under "Who to Follow" to find industries and companies that you need to keep updated about for your job search. Knowing the latest 'inside' information will speak volumes in an interview.

Tips and Techniques

Twitter Terms to Know

Tweet: The results of posting a message on Twitter. Messages are limited to 140 characters.

RT: A "retweet" is the result of posting another Twitter user's message on your own Twitter account, usually denoted by reposting the message and adding RT [username].

DM: Direct Message, which is a private message Twitter users can exchange. However, Direct Messages can only be exchanged if both users are following each other.

@Reply: A tweet that is public, but is directed at a specific user and is denoted by starting the tweet with the @ symbol and the individual's username.

Hashtag: A way to label conversations to make them easily categorized and searchable, denoted by using the "#" sign.

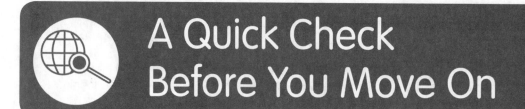

A Quick Check
Before You Move On

You need more than just a resume. In reality, you need a coordinated suite of communications tools, because you'll use them throughout your search. Career Resource Network (CRN) contains many resources and examples to help you put yours together.

Before you leave this milestone:
Go to Career Resource Network (CRN) to find:
- Samples of exit, positioning and accomplishment statements
- Hundreds of resumes, cover letters, follow-up letters and suggested email messages written and edited by professionals in their fields

When you're happy with your resume, you may post it on Resume Reserve, LHH's proprietary resume database on the CRN. This premium database can be found under "Quick Links" on the CRN website. This allows you to present your credentials to tens of thousands of registered human resources professionals. In addition, it provides you an opportunity to network with other individuals who can help you in your search.

You can find, contact and network with other individuals receiving LHH services who:
- Have worked at your target list companies
- Know about your function, industry or target geography
- Are colleagues from your previous employers, vendors or competitors
- Belong to your professional organizations or share your certifications
- Are experts in fields you're considering for a career change

Another LHH premium database service on the CRN is called JobScout, which allows you to see and collect job leads. Be sure to take advantage of the job tracking and notification features.

Milestone 4

Define Your Target Market

Why this Milestone is Important...

One of the most important (and often most neglected) aspects of search is clearly defining a target market – the market in which you will conduct your search.

Your Target Market Is the Group of Organizations You Plan to Pursue

One way to understand the value of defining a target market is to look at your search project as if it were a sales and marketing endeavor. If you were planning to introduce a new product, you would first need to identify the group of customers who would most likely need and purchase your product in order to focus your sales and marketing efforts. You would define that group using demographic factors such as age, income, gender and the like.

The same is true in job search. In search, your target market is defined by four factors: industry or type of organization, size, location and the culture of the organization.

Your Target Market Must Be Large Enough, but Manageable

Many people initially underestimate the number of targets they need for a successful search. Data collected by Lee Hecht Harrison indicates that the average person in search talks to 20 to 30 different hiring managers at 20 to 30 different organizations. Locating that many hiring managers generally requires starting with a target market much larger than 20 to 30 organizations.

If your target market is not large enough, you stand a chance of reducing your odds for success. This is analogous to fishing in a lake that contains only three fish. The odds of catching one fish are small. For this reason, we always recommend reality checking the size of your target market before proceeding with a full-blown search. This chapter describes a method for doing that.

On the other hand, having a target market that is too large also can present problems. People with hundreds or thousands of possibilities often run a search that is too diffuse and difficult to manage.

You Should Consider Where You Will Be Happy Working

In thinking about defining your target market, ask yourself two questions:

- *What organizations are most likely to be interested in someone like me?*

- *What organizations am I most interested in joining?*

Focusing your efforts on organizations that are most likely to be interested in someone like you increases your odds of landing a job more quickly. Focusing on organizations you really like increases the odds of your having satisfaction in your work and enthusiasm about your search.

As you do this milestone, think of it as an opportunity to select and target organizations that are most consistent with your career plans and personal preferences – organizations where you will be happy and satisfied.

This is worth some thought. After all, you will be spending a minimum of 40 hours a week with this particular group of people in this particular culture. Carefully defining your target market increases your odds of more quickly finding an organization in which you will be happy. Focusing on organizations you have hand picked provides an additional advantage: your authentic interest in these organizations makes you a more appealing candidate.

Why this Milestone is Important...

Your Target List Focuses Your Search

Once you have defined your target market, you need to make a list of the 50 most desirable targets in that market. A clearly defined target list focuses your search by helping you organize your day-to-day activities. In our experience, individuals who search without a target list tend to pursue opportunities more or less at random. This limits their chances of finding the best fit and often extends their search time.

With a target list, you will always have answers to the questions:

- *What will I do this week?*

- *Who will I talk to?*

- *What will I talk about?*

People effective in job search always are researching, talking to and talking about their top targets. They constantly improve and refine their target list, culling out less desirable targets and focusing more energy on the most desirable ones.

Your Target List Is a Central Topic of Conversation

All experts in search agree that informal conversations – or simply talking to people – is the single most effective way of locating appropriate new employment. Lee Hecht Harrison statistics show that most people talk to more than 100 different people in the course of a search.

What exactly do you say when you are talking to your contacts? Simply telling them that you are unemployed and looking for new employment might limit the conversation and make your contacts uncomfortable. Some career books suggest

asking for advice. However, unless you are making a major career change, you are probably already well informed on your industry. If you are someone with experience in your profession, asking for advice could present the wrong image and make you appear as less than a professional in your field.

However, making your target list the central topic of your conversations is not only useful to you, it makes your contacts more comfortable. Your contacts are usually happy to talk about organizations, especially ones where they have personal experience.

During the course of these conversations, you can get answers to some of your questions, such as:

- *Which organizations are friendliest to my particular profession?*

- *Which organizations have cultures that are most compatible with my own values?*

- *Which organizations are currently working on problems and issues that are of interest to me and compatible with my skills?*

Target Market Conversations Can Lead to Referrals

Having conversations about your targeted industries and companies – and their issues and opportunities – can prove to be highly productive for you. It is a very good way to augment the information you have acquired through your own research.

However, one of the most desirable outcomes of these conversations is that they can lead to introductions to new people, thereby expanding your search.

Questions to Explore

- *What geographic area do I prefer? Am I going to target all relevant companies in the world, just in particular countries, states/provinces and cities or within a specific commuting distance?*

- *What industry do I prefer? Which industries are likely to consider me a strong candidate?*

- *What size organization do I prefer? Will I measure the size of organizations by annual revenue, by number of employees or by other appropriate measures?*

- *What type of organizational culture do I prefer? What factors are important to me?*

- *Is it likely that a sufficient number of jobs will be opening up each month in my target market?*

- *Can I clearly describe my target market? If there are different segments to my market, can I describe my criteria for each?*

- *What resources will I use to build a list that is consistent with the target market criteria (location, industry and size) in my marketing plan? What resources will I use to get the information I need to prioritize the targets?*

- *How will I effectively use the Internet to do intensive research on my target market and target companies? Would membership in a social networking group be useful?*

Suggested Actions

- **Once you have established your criteria,** create a list of specific target organizations to explore by looking at resources such as the premium databases on the CRN and other business directories in the library and on the Internet.

- **Check to be sure your target list is large enough.** If the number of target organizations is not sufficient, you may need to review your target market definition, enlarge your geographic area, expand your objective, or increase the range of industries or size of companies.

- **If your target market consists of hundreds of organizations,** refine it and create a list of the 50 organizations that you will target initially.

- **Include the names, addresses, telephone numbers and emails of hiring managers** in your target list whenever possible, as well as any contacts you have in that industry or organization.

- **Prepare a personal marketing plan** that you can use to guide your search and to discuss with your contacts.

Evaluating Your Target Market

E stimate the answers to the questions based on your knowledge right now. Then, after you have conducted more research, add your actual numbers.

	Estimate	Actual Number
1. Number of organizations meeting geographic, industry and size criteria	_____	_____
2. Number of appropriate jobs (not openings) in each target company	_____	_____
3. Total number of jobs in this target market (number of organizations times number of jobs)	_____	_____
4. Number of years someone typically stays in one of these jobs	_____	_____
5. Number of openings each year (total number of jobs divided by number of years people stay)	_____	_____
6. Number of openings each month (yearly openings divided by 12)	_____	_____

Guidelines for Evaluating Your Target Market

When is your target market large enough? This is the critical question, because when a target market is too small, it can make your search longer. Once you have estimated the number of openings that might be available, the questions are: How many openings a month are enough? When is a target market large enough? When does it need to be expanded?

These are questions without simple answers because there are many considerations that must be factored into the equation. Following are some general guidelines:

If number of openings per month are...	then...
10 or less	seriously consider expanding your target market.
10 to 50	your target market is probably large enough.
Over 50	you have defined a target market that is large enough and you may need to select a smaller segment for a starting point.

Creating a Personal Marketing Plan

A sound, well-constructed personal marketing plan is key to ensuring that you focus on priority actions and avoid wasting time and energy on unproductive activities. As with any project, a good plan helps you organize and prioritize your work and keeps your productivity high. These pages are designed to help you create your personal marketing plan. Basically, there are four parts to creating a personal marketing plan.

Your Marketing Plan

1. Professional Objective with Preferred Functions

Referring back to the work you did in Milestone 2, your professional objective is a concise phrase or sentence that describes the kind of work you are seeking. It should reflect your values, traits, skills, interests, overall experience and expertise in a way that is clearly understood by people inside and outside of your profession. This simple sentence form is especially effective if you choose to put it on your resume.

A variation of this is the professional objective with preferred functions, which may serve you better in creating your marketing plan.

After your professional objective, you will want to include your functions – the role or areas of work that fit your experience and interest. Normally, this consists of one or two words and should include 3-5 targeted functions. Functions can be displayed as a list under the professional objective. You should be able to name job titles typical of these functions and combinations of them.

SAMPLES
Marketing Management
- strategy development
- product development
- market research

Senior Banker
- commercial banking
- branch banking
- special asset liquidation
- compliance
- asset management

Senior Electrical Design Engineer
- telecom and datacom
- leading hardware teams
- product development

2. Positioning Statement with Competency List

The positioning statement you created in Milestone 3 is meant to be spoken. It also could be called your skills summary or what you can do for a prospective employer. For use in your marketing plan, you need to convert your spoken positioning statement into a written one. This simply involves pulling the competencies out of the spoken positioning statement and converting them into a written list.

Competency list

In Milestone 2, you compiled a list of your competencies, or clusters of skills and personal characteristics. These are the areas in which you have experience or particular expertise. Sometimes competencies are very generic (i.e., teamwork); sometimes they also can be very specific (i.e., ISO 14000). A good list usually has both. The best way to list your competencies in a marketing plan is to use 3-6 headings or categories that effectively title the areas of expertise.

You should be able to tell at least one brief accomplishment story to illustrate each of your competencies. Using accomplishment stories to emphasize competencies is a powerful and memorable way to make your case, both in interviews and when talking to inside contacts before interviewing.

3. Target Market	4. Target List
Your target market defines the types of organizations you plan to pursue. Your criteria for defining your target market needs to include the following four elements: • **Geographic Location -** The first criterion in identifying your target market is geographic location. Will you pursue all relevant companies in the country of your choice? Or, are you limiting yourself to within a commuting distance of your current residence? Location is determined by personal preferences and by market demand. Define your geographic preference in a way that it can be drawn on a map, like a sales territory. • **Industry or Type of Organization -** The second criterion is industry or type of organization. Again, part of this is a matter of personal preference. For some, the professional objective and qualifications dictate the industry. A metallurgist will work in primary metals and metal products. Another critical factor is how much your past experience will determine if you will be seen as a strong candidate. A financial professional with manufacturing experience is seen as a strong candidate in manufacturing. • **Size of Organization -** The size of an organization usually is defined either in terms of annual revenue or number of employees. For some, size is a matter of personal preference. It can be a critical factor. Below a certain size a company may not have the position you are seeking. For example, a company of only 200 employees is not likely to hire an HR director for six figures. • **Organizational Culture -** Organization culture is sometimes a factor in determining a target market. Generally, however, it is not used to determine the initial list, but to help prioritize the target companies.	**Once you have developed your criteria, the last component of your marketing plan is an initial target list of 50 organizations.** You can identify these initial companies by researching resources such as the premium databases on the CRN and other business directories in the library and online. Use a disciplined process when identifying target companies to be sure that you consider all viable targets.

Your Marketing Plan

Elements of the Target Market

• **Geographic location of organization:** stated precisely enough that you could draw it on a map, like a sales territory.

• **Industry or type of organization:** identified by the Standard Industrial Classification (SIC) or North American Industry Classification System (NAICS) codes.

• **Size of organization:** stated in annual revenue, number of employees or other measures appropriate to your industry or profession.

• **Organizational culture:** stated concretely enough to research targets, e.g., an organization with more than 20% women at all levels or an organization that routinely uses cross-functional teams.

SAMPLE

One-Page Marketing Plan

Name
Address / City / State / Zip
Telephone Number
Email Address

Senior Environmental, Health & Safety Manager

Regulatory Affairs	Internal EH&S Consulting/Advising
Compliance Auditing	EH&S Management

Positioning Statement

Experienced in advising management, directing programs and personnel, managing national and international remediation projects and conducting corporate-wide compliance audits in both Fortune 500 companies and small consulting firms. I have managed projects and departments, conducted acquisition and divestiture reviews, set direction for EH&S policy and delivered results affecting the bottom line. Competencies include:

Management	Auditing	Remediation	Training
Internal/external staffing	ISO 14000	Site assessment	EH&S program leader
Communications	Corporate program development	Regulatory agencies	Audit team leader
Group productivity	Corporate program tracking	Consultant bid process	Site audit program
Coaching	Corrective action	Investigative technologies	Site instructor
Leading teams	Follow-through	Testing lab issues	

Target Market with Sample Target Companies

Geographic area: NJ, NY and CT within a radius of 35 miles from zip code 07013. **Types of industries:** chemical and pharmaceutical manufacturing; consulting firms. **Size of organizations:** manufacturing – more than 1,000 employees; consulting – any size.

Pharmaceuticals	Chemicals	Consultants
Aquatics Pharmaceuticals Corporation	Alpha Corp.	Chemicals Management, Inc.
Berringer Laboratories, Inc.	Amaroco Incorporated	Concurrent Medical Centers
Creskill, Inc.	B & J Biosciences	Cybertechnical Group, Inc.
Forum Laboratories, Inc.	BAK Gases Inc.	Edgarson International
Garden State Laboratories, Inc.	Croton, Inc.	Gomez-Koffman, P.C.
Merris Limited	EcoBioSphere Corp.	Henry Drabble Associates
OrganicTron, Inc.	Exact Chemicals, Inc.	IZ Radiation Protection, Inc.
Patson, Inc.	General Chemical Corporation	L. Bonifanti Engineering, Inc.
Pharmaceutica Corporation	Hartford Specialty Chemicals	Larriff Associates
	ITC Specialty Products	McCauley Associates, Inc.

Your Marketing Plan

Implementing Your Marketing Plan

Here are ideas on how to implement your marketing plan in the most effective manner:

Implement Plan A and Plan B Simultaneously

A good marketing plan is often a combination of a plan A and a plan B. The most common example of this is wanting to work within commuting range of your current home (plan A), but willing to relocate if necessary (plan B).

People in search often make the mistake of conducting A and B in sequence, moving to plan B only if plan A fails to produce results. This can waste time and effort and, even more damaging, risk making a bad impression on their contacts.

If you have relocation as plan B, but initially pursue only plan A, telling your contacts you are looking only locally may create problems. If you later decide to go to plan B, you will need to reconnect with your contacts to get information on the additional target organizations – information you could have gotten at your first meeting.

This kind of change also might create the impression that your local search has failed or your qualifications are weaker than you thought. It is more productive and less risky to cover both plans A and B the first time, perhaps allocating 60% of your time each week to A and 40% to B, and always talking to your contacts about both.

Pursue Your Top Targets Each Week

Consider setting weekly goals based on your plan. For instance, get enough information on five of your top 10 targets to determine whether or not you would be happy working there, or talk to three insiders at your top 10 targets, or add five new organizations to your list this week.

Refine Your Target List Regularly

Revisit your marketing plan on a regular basis and refine it based on what you have learned in your conversations with contacts. As you gather information, reprioritize your target list each week. Some targets will rise to the top of your list and get even more attention next week. Others will fall to the bottom of the list and get less effort. You are likely to add new targets, as well. By proceeding this way, you increase your chances of landing at an organization that you know well and really like.

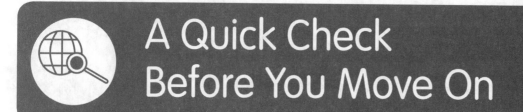

A Quick Check
Before You Move On

The trick to Defining Your Target Market is in defining criteria that work for you personally – that align with your objectives, not anyone else's. Once you have established your criteria (taking into account the geography, industry, size, and culture you want), you can create a list of specific target organizations to explore by tapping into resources such as databases and other business directories in your library and on the Internet. Career Resource Network (CRN) provides access to many of these.

Before you leave this milestone:

Go to Career Resource Network (CRN) to find tools to help you build, calculate and evaluate your target market, including ways to:

*   Research employers via links to databases and other sources
*   Create your marketing plan using the marketing plan template and the sample marketing plans (which vary by industry and job title)

As a final step within this milestone, check to be sure your target list is large enough. If the number of target organizations is not sufficient, you may need to review your target market definition, enlarge your geographic area, expand your objective, increase the range of industries or adjust the size of the companies you're targeting.

Implement search

Measure your progress

Implement Search

The Implementation Phase of the AIM process includes Milestones 5 through 8, and usually includes additional work on Milestone 1.

Progress measurements in this phase can be done with the LHH Job Search Productivity Chart, which can be found on the CRN under Sample Documents in the Quick Links. This chart is done in a daily format, allowing you to keep close watch on your progress.

Milestone	Outcome	Pages
5. Gather Marketplace Information	**You have a continuing flow of current information about target organizations** from people (preferably insiders) who are knowledgeable about those organizations, and you are conducting background research so that you can relate your assets to their needs.	71-84
6 Get Your Message Out	**You are having search-related conversations** (during which you mention your qualifications) with 20 to 30 people a week on a continual basis, gathering information about your target industries/organizations and identifying hiring managers.	85-106
7. Talk with Hiring Managers	**You are thoroughly prepared to answer difficult questions**, you have prepared your own questions to ask, and you are having meaningful conversations with two new hiring managers a week.	107-120
8. Consider Other Methods of Search	**You are responding to appropriate ads or jobs posted on the Internet on a regular basis,** and the recruiters or agencies you have contacted are sending you on interviews. Or you have determined that these methods are not appropriate for you, in which case you will need to concentrate on talking directly to hiring managers.	121-136

Milestone 5

Gather Marketplace Information

Why this Milestone is Important...

As the old adage says, knowledge is power. Knowledge – the right knowledge – about your marketplace and your target organizations gives you significant power. Having marketplace information allows you to:

- **Make better decisions about your own work life and career.**
- **Create a better impression when talking to people about job opportunities.**
- **Gain entrance to people who otherwise might not talk to you.**
- **Induce people to invite you back for further discussion.**
- **Wield extraordinary leverage in interviews and salary negotiations.**

In spite of all of this, effective information gathering continues to be one of the most neglected areas of search, even with the ease of access to knowledge made possible by computer databases and Internet information sources.

You Need to Use Three Sources of Information: Printed, Online and People

There are three sources typically used to gather marketplace information by people in search. The first and simplest source is printed materials. Newspapers, especially the business pages, offer the most current information, as do specialized industry and professional newspapers and trade journals.

Online sources provide the capability of conducting searches on industries, companies and professions in a faster and more convenient way than printed sources, if you know how to use them effectively.

There are, however, distinct limitations to the information available in print or online since some information is simply never publicly recorded. The third source of information is talking to people who have personal knowledge about your industry, profession and target companies. Virtually all experts in search agree that talking to people is a key element in search success. In many cases, information found in print and online can serve as a starting point for these conversations.

You Need Information to Prioritize Your Target List

By this milestone, you have completed your marketing plan, which includes a target list of approximately 50 organizations. Your next step is to begin the process of gathering information about those targets so that you can prioritize your list and determine how to best allocate your efforts. We suggest you begin with your 10 top target organizations.

As part of your research, you will determine whether a target company meets your criteria as a place where you would like to work, and whether it ever employs people with your talents and experience. As part of this process, you may find that some of the organizations on your initial target list do not warrant your time and effort and can be removed from your list and replaced by more viable organizations. You also will begin to identify prime targets that deserve more of your attention.

Why this Milestone is Important...

You Need Information to Pursue Your Top Targets

Once you have made preliminary decisions about your top targets, you can begin to collect more in-depth information about your industry, your profession or function and your target companies, paying particular attention to the current issues, trends and problems they are encountering.

- **Industry information:** Collecting information on your industry (or industries) as a whole not only positions you as someone with in-depth industry knowledge, but also helps you compare companies within a given industry so that you can identify the leaders and the laggards. This is valuable information you can use as you hone down and add to your target list. In addition, information you gathered earlier on industry compensation practices could give you an enormous advantage later when you are negotiating an offer.

- **Professional information:** As part of your research, you also need to look for information about your particular profession, function or area of expertise – again looking at current trends, issues and problems that are affecting your profession at the moment or might in the near future.

- **Target company information:** Having a thorough knowledge of your individual target companies positions you as someone who might be able to offer solutions to the challenges they are facing. Being seen as someone with valuable knowledge can enhance your ability to gain access to key people and hiring managers.

You Need Information to Be Effective in Search Conversations

As mentioned in the chapter for Milestone 4, people are more comfortable talking with you about companies, industries or functions than they are about your employment situation. Being armed with up-to-date and in-depth knowledge allows you to engage in truly meaningful conversations with insiders and hiring managers and ultimately presents you as an appealing candidate.

Information is the currency of search. Because you will be continually researching and collecting information, you just might be more current than your conversation partners. Providing information about competitors or current issues might make you a valuable resource to them, someone they would welcome a conversation with and invite back for more discussion. Obviously, you need to use discretion when sharing information you acquired as a result of talking to insiders, particularly if you agreed to treat the information as confidential.

As you become more skilled in having these search conversations, you will develop your overall networking skills. While the information you gather at this stage is the critical thing, it is the practice of talking to people about issues, industries and trends that prepares you to get out and meet more people.

Questions to Explore

- *Which organizations are likely to meet both my personal criteria (location, size and type) and have a need for someone with my talents and experience?*

- *What do my target organizations do? What are their business strategies? What challenges are they facing that might require my competencies and expertise? Who are their competitors? What can I find out about their culture?*

- *What departments, units or job titles am I best suited for in each of the organizations? What resources will I use to find the names, emails and phone numbers of the managers and other key contacts?*

- *Who are the key people – perhaps leaders of industry organizations or lobbying groups – who have extensive knowledge of the industries I am targeting? Who are the key people in the individual organizations I am targeting? Who are the relevant hiring managers?*

- *What are the compensation practices at my level in my chosen industries? What is the going rate for someone at my level with my competencies? How is compensation usually structured for the job titles that interest me?*

Suggested Actions

- **Collect additional information on your target organizations and other potential targets** by showing your list to appropriate networking contacts. Make a habit of asking questions about your target organizations in every conversation you have about work.

- **Compile a list of questions to ask people inside target organizations** so that you are always prepared and have a way to get people talking.

- **Although your primary focus should be on gathering information from sources in your business community,** continue to research target organizations by reading articles in newspapers, magazines and trade journals and by checking the Internet sites of organizations for marketing information and annual reports.

- **Consider joining (or revisiting) social networking sites** such as LinkedIn, Facebook or any of the emerging "niche" sites for any information that your contacts may provide.

- **Set up a system for retaining and organizing the large amount of research you will be collecting**.

- **Continue to survey your professional environment by:**
  1. **Talking to people currently engaged in the work you are considering** to be certain you have the qualifications for the work defined by your professional objective.
  2. **Attending professional or industry association meetings and talking with people in your profession** to get their perspectives on what is changing.
  3. **Discussing your analysis of your profession and industry with peers**, both inside and outside your profession and industry.

- **Evaluate the volume and reliability of the information you have on each target** as if you were making a major investment decision.

Gather Information in a Logical Sequence

There is a logical sequence to doing research so that you capture the information you need in a way that makes it immediately useful to you. Sometimes you will come upon valuable information at unexpected times and from surprising sources. Whatever the sources, you must have a process to manage your overall research. A useful model for conducting your research is shown in the following box:

The Sequence of Research

1. **Develop the best questions to ask.** You need to determine exactly what you need to know. One way to make this determination is to develop questions. You can use the questions listed under Questions to Explore in each milestone chapter as a starting point. You also will want to develop questions that are specific to your marketing plan, your target organizations and the kind of positions you plan to pursue.

2. **Conduct your research in the most time-efficient manner.** Finding your next position is primarily a process of contacting people. The information you uncover in your research can serve to facilitate the conversations you have with your contacts. Conduct your research as efficiently as possible and then move on to having conversations.

3. **Share information with your network of acquaintances.** Share your information and knowledge with others to test its accuracy and to seek out additional information. Whenever possible, reciprocate by providing your contacts with information useful to them and their careers. Joining and actively participating in an Internet-based social networking site can help with this and with point 2.

4. **Take action on the information.** Use your research to locate and meet new people, start new conversations and continue conversations with existing contacts. Information that has no actionable use actually may slow down your efforts.

There are three main areas of research you will want to pursue: your industry, target companies and issues. The following pages investigate these three areas further.

Productivity Pointer

Organize your online resources

Internet browsers allow you to create bookmarks (or favorite places) so you can return to helpful sites quickly and easily. Within these bookmarks, you can organize your collection of search-related Web links into folders for even quicker access. If you have found a website that is particularly useful in your search, bookmark it so you can access it with one click. You may wish to bookmark the websites of all your top targets as well.

Researching Your Industry

Researching your industry provides a context for assessing individual target organizations. This research also verifies or corrects your perception of your industry. Be prepared to reassess your career goal in light of what you discover. Emerging industry trends have the potential to limit or enhance your career. Your command of current industry information makes you an attractive conversation partner to the insiders you want to meet.

Here are some basic questions to guide you when researching your industry:

- *What organizations comprise my industry?*

- *What are the overall trends, challenges and opportunities that will have an effect on them?*

- *What innovations in the industry may signal changes ahead?*

- *Are my career goals consistent with what is happening in the industry?*

- *Is my current industry choice still the best choice? What others may be possible choices?*

- *Who are the major players in my targeted geographical area? How do they differ? How are they the same?*

- *What issues do each of them face? Are the issues the same or different?*

How to Research Your Industry

A great deal of industry information can be acquired through reading industry journals, trade magazines and news articles on companies within an industry. In conducting industry research, Standard Industrial Classification (SIC) codes or North American Industry Classification System (NAICS) codes can be useful:

- **Identify appropriate SIC or NAICS codes** by looking up the code for your former employer or an organization you know you could work for. Use those codes to identify other appropriate industries. If you cannot find a code for industries you have in mind, get assistance.

- **Include on your list industries you know nothing about,** but would like to investigate further. Much can be learned by including questions that are industry-specific, based on what you have learned through your networking conversations. Questions about trends are particularly important when talking with industry insiders.

 **Productivity Pointer**

Collect industry information as you go.
As you collect and research information on your specific target companies in the same industry, you will begin to develop a picture of that industry as a whole. You are then in a position to compare your target companies to the industry leaders. You also will be completing the survey of your professional and industry environment you began in Milestone 1.

Researching a Target Company

Before initiating any contact with your targeted organizations, you need to be prepared to present yourself in the most effective way possible and to explore how you might best contribute to a particular organization. This requires constantly researching your top 10 targets. This will not only prepare you for an interview, but also will give you the ammunition you need to get the interview in the first place.

Perhaps most important of all, you will have the information you need to make an informed choice about what organization you will ultimately join and how to prioritize your search efforts in the meantime. Think carefully about what you already know about an organization and what you need to uncover. Asking good questions is the toughest (but most important) part of research.

Here are some basic questions to guide you when researching your target companies:

- *What is the full name of the organization? Where is it located? How large is it (in terms of revenue, number of employees and product lines)?*

- *What industry is it in? What products does it make or what services does it provide?*

- *How long has it been in business? What has its growth pattern been? How well is it doing right now?*

- *Who are the competitors? Where does the company stand in its industry?*

- *Who are the key executives? Who are the hiring managers?*

- *What needs does this organization have that I might be able to fill? (If you have not read anything explicit on this subject, what inferences can you make?)*

How to Research a Target Company

- **Get a copy of the annual report or 10K** for each of your target companies by mail or through their websites.

- **Stay current** by reading newspapers and journals. Be alert for articles on companies in the industries you are targeting. Ask friends to keep their eyes open for articles on your targets.

- **Use online resources.** Career Resource Network provides access to several databases that can help you with information about the companies you are interested in.

- **Have specific questions ready.** Exactly what do you want to know?

- **Bookmark and review the individual websites of your target organizations.** Make sure you go to their employment or job listings frequently.

The outcome of your research: knowing enough to decide where to place the organization on your target list (or eliminate it from consideration) and to interview well when the opportunity arises.

Researching the Issues

Researching the current issues in organizations, industries and professions can help you prioritize your target list by identifying organizations likely to need what you have to offer. It also can make networking easier by identifying people who share your interests and by giving you more information to offer your networking contacts.

An example of this kind of research is the human resources professional, with experience in self-directed work teams, who researches the use of work teams. Articles on self-directed work teams may reveal the names of organizations and people using such teams. They also may reveal organizational needs relating to teams and information on who is succeeding with teams (and who is not) and why.

How to Research the Issues

- **Conduct a literature search** on the issue or topic you are trying to learn about. The Web should provide a wealth of information. Your library is a good source, too.

- **Determine if there are any websites** devoted specifically to your topic. However, use caution – try to determine the origin, authority and date of any information you find on the Web.

- **Identify an industry or trade association** that is likely to have information about the issue you are investigating. Call the association to see what information it can provide or direct you to.

- **Identify and contact experts** on a topic, such as people who are quoted in articles, who have written or spoken on the topic, who teach courses on the topic (determine which colleges have degree-granting programs that might include your topic) and others who also might be conducting research on the topic.

- **Finally, be very familiar with the issues** facing your target companies. You need to have a good sense of these issues so that you can speak intelligently to their needs. Being focused on the issues facing your target companies will make you an informed conversation partner with inside contacts and a more attractive candidate in actual interviews.

Tips and Techniques

Blogging is a trend being used on both sides of job search.
When researching a company, company blogs can provide useful information about a company. However, you always need to keep the veracity and possible intent of the source in mind.

Some companies encourage employee blogging (and may pay employees to do it). To head off negative or confidential information from getting out, many companies now require that anything said about a company by an employee in a blog be approved in advance.

Should you blog? Some employers use blogs as a prescreening device so be cautious of anything you write in any blog you post. It might come back to haunt you.

Sources for Marketplace Information

Online Resources

Online information sources can be a faster and more convenient way of collecting information than paper sources.

- If you know how to use them effectively, online services can quickly make you an expert on narrow topics of information.

- You can conduct searches on industries, companies, issues, problems, successes and people.

- If you are able to stay focused in your efforts – rather than get lost in surfing – you can do this quite quickly.

Lee Hecht Harrison's Career Resource Network (CRN) has been designed to provide you with the best possible tools to accomplish your goal and accumulate information that is practical, accessible and actionable.

Additional online resources

- The Internet is an invaluable resource if you have thoughtfully laid out your research, know what you are looking for and know how to conduct a search.

- Corporate websites, job posting sites and other information sources are abundant.

Alternative Sources

- **The library.** A valuable, but often neglected, information resource is the local library. Reference librarians are trained to manage the resources and methods for finding information within their facility and through exchange privileges with other libraries. When using library resources, use the same rules as for all other research:

  - Develop good questions so that you can describe to the librarian what you need and why.

  - Think through how you are going to use the information. Will you use it to develop a list, prioritize your targets, use it in an interview? The librarian needs this information to assist you.

  - Look for data that is most useful. Avoid approaches such as: I need to know everything about Amalgamated Corporation. The truth is, you don't need to know everything about this organization. Think in terms of you and your work.

Productivity Pointer

Internet: Friend or Foe?

Lee Hecht Harrison consultants sometimes notice candidates spending inordinate amounts of time surfing the Internet. When asked how they have advanced their search in the last hour (or two or six), some of the candidates are unable to give an answer. The Internet is a powerful information tool when used in a focused way, but it can also be a serious distraction from productive work.

As a general rule, never spend more than 30 minutes online at one sitting. Have well-defined questions prepared before you turn on the computer. Get your answers and act on them! Don't fall into the trap of long, unproductive searches that lead you away from your objective.

Gathering Information from Your Personal Contacts

One of the best sources of up-to-date marketplace information is within the marketplace itself. Our statistics show that people in search often have 300 conversations with more than 100 different people in the course of a search. Most of these conversations are not interviews; they are opportunities to collect inside information about your industry, your target companies and the people within your industry. The best place to start having such conversations is with the people with whom you are most comfortable: your friends and acquaintances.

Conversations With Friends and Acquaintances

One of the reasons people give for avoiding search-related conversations with friends and acquaintances is they feel as if they are asking for a favor. The truth is that these conversations, especially at this stage of the process, allow you to tap into the information your contacts have and to refine and sharpen your overall strategy. If you never get a job lead from these conversations, you will still gain from them because knowledge picked up in this way will advance your search.

A dialogue with a friend might go like this:

You: *Nicole, I'd like to get together with you to talk about my career transition.*

Nicole: *I really don't know of anybody hiring right now so I'm not sure I can help.*

You: *I appreciate your wanting to help, Nicole, but I'm not asking about any openings. What I'm interested in right now is your reaction to the marketing plan I have put together to guide my search. In particular, I have a list of target companies I'm gathering information on. I don't know if any of them are currently hiring, but sooner or later one of them will, and I plan to be ready for that. I have 50 companies on the list, and I'm guessing that you know something about some of them. Would you be willing to take a look?*

Questions to Fill in Gaps in Your Research

Once you have developed information from online databases, books and magazines, you need to fill in the gaps. Talking to people about your research allows you to validate or learn new details.

A sample dialogue with a friend might be:

You: *Michael, I've been researching the Saxony Industrial group. I noticed that Saxony's product line overlaps with your company's. Are they a competitor?*

Michael: *Yes, on certain product lines, but recently they have not been a strong competitor. We're much more concerned with Thorpe Industries and the Morse Group these days.*

You: *That's very interesting. Does Saxony have problems or just a few weak products? Can you tell me a bit more about all three companies?*

Use Your Research with Your Network Contacts

When researching several companies in the same industry, you are also gathering valuable competitive information, such as industry issues and particular companies and people. This information can be useful and valuable to your network contacts. (Remember to use discretion when sharing information, especially if it has come from insiders.)

A sample dialogue might be:

You: *Ms. Diaz, I am a friend of Michael Watson's. He suggested that I talk with you because I'm working on a career move. As part of that effort, I've been collecting information on companies in your industry, including Thorpe, Morse and Saxony. Michael told me you are in sales and are selling to all three and that you might be interested in hearing what I've learned. And, I would be very interested in any information you might be willing to share on these and other companies on my target list. Would you be interested in hearing what I've learned?*

Ms. Diaz: *Yes, I would be very interested in hearing what you have learned.*

Fine-Tune Your Research Questions

Finally, of course, you will focus in on your particular department or area of interest inside the company. What are they doing? Who is doing it? How effective are their efforts? The more you can find out on these topics, the more appealing a candidate you become. You also become better able to focus on your skills and strengths in your presentation, tying what you can do to what they need. Naturally, all of this is of great value when you get the opportunity to talk to hiring managers.

A sample dialogue with a friend might go like this:

You: *Fred, with my background, I am considering either a position as a corporate training manager or starting my own training consulting business. I am trying to get a better understanding of how various organizations manage the training function and their selection and use of outside vendors. I know you used to work as a training manager at United Amalgamated. Would you be willing to talk to me about how they do things in training Departments?*

Fred: *Yes. I'd be happy to. We conducted about 25% of our training using inside trainers and contracted with about a dozen different vendors for the rest. Exactly what would you like to know?*

Using Your Marketplace Information

Gathering information about your marketplace is an important, ongoing process that can have an impact on every phase of your search project.

Marketplace Information and Career Objectives

As part of your work in Milestone 1, you researched your professional environment to determine how much opportunity exists in your field, where your career might go and what professional development you might need, if any. This marketplace information helped you initially formulate your professional objective. As you continue to gather information, you might find it useful to refine your objective.

Marketplace Information and Communication Strategy

Your resume and other communications need to be effective and compelling. Marketplace research allows you to keep current on the language of your marketplace as it evolves, so that you are able to incorporate language that is meaningful to today's hiring managers into your communications strategy. In addition, research keeps you current on the problems, issues and opportunities in the industry so that you can present yourself as knowledgeable about some or all of them.

Marketplace Information and the Marketing Plan

The information you continue to gather as part of your work on this milestone offers you an opportunity to ensure that your marketing plan continues to point you in the right direction. As you research target companies, you may find that some on your initial list are no longer appropriate, or that other new companies need to be added. Having a continuing stream of information about your marketplace helps you keep your search focused.

Marketplace Information and Networking

Having relevant information about your marketplace is crucial to your effectiveness and success in networking. As a result of your solid research efforts, you are able to exchange information with your contacts in a way that is meaningful and helpful to you and to them.

Marketplace Information and Interviewing

Simply stated, a hiring manager is looking for the one person, among several qualified candidates, who is the best fit for the job. One of the best impressions you can give is that you are well-informed about the industry, your profession and that particular organization. Further, this information helps you develop insightful questions to ask in the interview.

Marketplace Information and Negotiating Salary

As you continue to gather information, you will also get a better feel for your value in the marketplace and become better prepared for salary negotiations. Your research into published information on compensation practices, along with your discussion about compensation with your networking contacts, will make you a stronger negotiator.

Productivity Pointer

Do you know who might know?

When pursuing marketplace information with friends and acquaintances, always ask for referrals to additional people with information. Any time your contact does not have information you need, ask: *Do you know someone who might have that information?* In addition to locating the information, you may be able to meet another contact. Internet-based social networking sites offer excellent opportunities to leverage your contacts.

Organizing Your Marketplace Information

Y ou are likely to accumulate a large body of information as you proceed with your search project. Decide early on how you will manage the information you are accumulating so it will be easily accessible when you need it. Included with your materials are tracking documents for your target companies, networking contacts and overall productivity (See the Search Project Organizer on the CRN). You also might consider using a binder, personal digital assistant or contact management/database software. Following are some suggestions on what to include:

Contact Management

- Records of your general contacts (when you spoke, topics of conversation)
- Records of your contacts with target companies (when you spoke, topics of conversation)
- Telephone list of your key contacts
- Email address book
- Recruiter list

Published Openings

- Positions you have applied for (open a research file and keep a record of contacts)
- Copies of all related correspondence

Research

- Files on targeted organizations, industry information and key people

Copies of Documents

- Your resume
- Your marketing plan
- Your reference list
- Licenses, your publication list, portfolio or other relevant documents

 **Productivity Pointer**

How do you know that?

How do you know that? is a great question to ask when someone provides useful information on a targeted organization. Sometimes the response is simply: *I don't know.* But more often you will learn of a useful new information source. With a little bit of luck, the response is the name of a person – perhaps even an insider or a hiring manager – whom your contact can introduce you to.

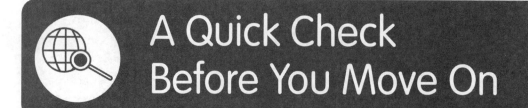

A Quick Check Before You Move On

You will continually gather marketplace information throughout your search, and you will use it in networking, interviewing and negotiating. You will eliminate certain organizations as you learn more about them, and you'll add others based on your evolving criteria. Information is key, whether the source is printed matter, Internet resources or the people you talk with.

Before you leave this milestone:

Go to Career Resource Network (CRN) to find:

- Tips on how to research industries, target companies and issues.
- The LHH Search Project Organizer, which will help you stay organized and on track. Download and get familiar with it. Save it to your hard drive and begin to use it.

Once you have a target list, try compiling a "stock" list and sequence of questions to ask people in your networking efforts. If you do this, you'll always have a way to get people talking and providing you the information you want.

And set up a computer-based system for retaining and organizing the large amount of research you will be collecting. Open up some new folders on your hard drive for this, and name them "Industry," "Companies," and "Issues." As your search progresses, you'll want separate files for each of the organizations you're pursuing.

Milestone 6

Get Your Message Out

Why this Milestone is Important...

By the time you've reached this milestone, you have accomplished quite a bit. You have a communications strategy in place and have developed a solid, workable marketing plan. However, in spite of all your work, you may be one of the best-kept secrets around. It is comparable to having created one of the world's best advertising campaigns but having no media plan for its dissemination. You need to get your message out about your qualifications and availability, and we have a suggestion on how to broadcast it.

Word-of-Mouth Advertising Is Essential in Search

How many times have you bought a product or hired a vendor based on the recommendations of a friend? People talking to people is still one of the most effective forms of advertising – even in our sometimes complicated and highly technical culture. Most businesses know that, in spite of massive advertising and promotion, word-of-mouth advertising is a formidable marketing channel. It can kill a product in the marketplace – or be responsible for its success. The same is true in conducting an effective search: You need to get your message out – consistently, frequently and to as many people as possible. You will do this through letters and resumes, but the single most effective way is by talking to people.

Integrate Your Message into Conversations

A problem in using word-of-mouth advertising in search is that you are the primary carrier of the message and might look egotistical – or even a bit odd – if you deliver a strong, positive message about yourself and your career strengths in the wrong way. For instance, imagine saying:

Good morning, Susan. I am a General Manager of Service Businesses and very good at turning around those with profitability problems. Well, see you later. Have a nice day.

The solution to this problem is to integrate your well-prepared message into conversations, typically combining it with discussions of your search and discussions of marketplace information as described in Milestone 5. This milestone presents systems and structures for accomplishing this.

Influence How Your Message Gets Out

The fact is that you are a topic of conversation among people who know you right now. You cannot control that. People talk about what they see and hear. People also talk about people they know, covering both positives and negatives. You cannot control that, but you can influence how the conversation goes by getting out a clear message, which will end up incorporated into their conversations.

Imagine, for instance, someone who knows you saying this about you:

I saw Keith yesterday. He looks great. He left United Amalgamated in that merger, but it didn't seem to bother him a bit. He seems certain that his next job will be a step up in his career. He's talking about medical products companies and is going after some fast-growth companies. Did you know he doubled sales at UA and in another company? UA even gave him an award.

When the message comes out positive, it is certainly because you provided the information, effectively using your exit statement, positioning statement and target list information. If you do not get your message out, people are likely to create their own story, and it will not be nearly as effective as yours. When you get your message out effectively, you enable others to make useful connections for you.

Get Your Message Out in a Natural Way

Happily, your central search message is one that fits into normal social conversations.

People often start these conversations with a question such as: *What's up?* Those who have heard about your former company's merger, acquisition, reorganization or downsizing might start with something more explicit.

Why this Milestone is Important...

Here is how to answer and get your message out:

1. *I left United Amalgamated, and I am very excited about my search for a new general manager position with P & L responsibility – and possibly a turnaround opportunity.*

2. *This is natural since my background includes _____, _____ and _____.*

3. *Some of the places I am particularly interested in are _____, _____ and _____. The _____ industry interests me and the _____ industry is also possible.*

4. *I've made up a list of organizations I want to investigate as possible next employers. Would you be willing to take a look at the list and see if you know anything about any of them?*

Your answer can stop after 3 or 4. But if you stop sooner, you are not getting your message out effectively.

Talking with People is a Natural Way to Get Your Message Out

A common objection to talking to friends and acquaintances in search is:

I don't want to ask for help. I don't want to burden my friends, so I'm not telling them I'm in transition.

As we saw in Milestone 5, meeting with people to gather marketplace information is beneficial to the careers of you and your contacts. By giving your friends the right message about yourself, you also might put them in a position to do a favor for one of their acquaintances by producing a qualified candidate at no charge. Some organizations even pay a bonus to employees who do this. And, if you have done Milestone 5 effectively and gathered useful market-place information, you may provide information that can help your contact as much as they help you.

In fact, this kind of information exchange is part of normal human interaction. We call it relationship networking, and in this section we will discuss its use in attaining the goals of Milestones 5 and 6.

The truth is that people who are effective in search talk to large numbers of people, typically more than 100 different people. There are many advantages to devoting the majority of your search time talking to people. We have enumerated them in this section.

The Call from "Out of the Blue"

At Lee Hecht Harrison, we have often heard people in search talk about a call they got "out of the blue" that resulted in a great lead or an interview. These people are nearly always people who have conducted excellent searches where they have effectively gotten their message out to many people, who in turn have passed it on to many others. The call from "out of the blue" is actually the result of earlier work in getting the message out to some of the right people.

Even if you have a touch of the I'm-not-going-to-bother-my-friends syndrome, do yourself and them a favor and get your message out. Word-of-mouth advertising works. Do it tastefully and effectively. And do it a lot.

Productivity Pointer

According to sociologists, this method, usually called networking, is how the majority of people find jobs. It usually involves what sociologist Mark Granovetter famously called "the strength of weak connections," or talking to people you know well to meet people you know less well (the "weak connections"), who introduce you to hiring managers.

The use of the Internet is on the rise, particularly with larger (10,000+ employees) organizations. These employers continue to see high value in employee referrals, but also make use of their own corporate websites and other Internet sources, as well as conventional sources like recruiters and newspapers.

Questions to Explore

- *Who do I know in any of my target organizations?*

- *Who among my family and friends would be willing to review my target list and provide me with information about the organizations or the names of people who work there?*

- *Who among my professional and industry contacts and former colleagues can I contact for information, referrals and ideas?*

- *Am I listed on a social networking site? How can I leverage this resource?*

- *What professional and industry associations am I involved with or can I get involved with to demonstrate my knowledge and skills and meet people who might be helpful?*

- *Who has been a source of career guidance in the past that I could discuss my targets with?*

Suggested Actions

- **Make a list of people you can contact initially**, starting with the people you know and who are easy to talk to, and begin to contact them by phone and in person. Continue to expand your list by adding at least 10 new people a week.

- **Consider joining (or revisiting) social networking sites** or any of the emerging "niche" sites for any information that your contacts may provide.

- **In addition to getting your message out, use these contacts to continue to gather marketplace information.** Use the SMART method to discuss your marketing plan and target list, as appropriate.

- **Attend professional association meetings and take an active role on a special project or committee.** Keep your skills fresh while demonstrating your capabilities to contacts.

- **If you like public speaking, find opportunities to share your expertise with others** while making your name and capabilities more visible in the marketplace.

- **Follow up with your contacts on a regular basis,** letting them know of your progress in general and reporting back to them on the results of referrals they may have given you.

- **Visit a bookstore, library (or an online bookseller) and find a few good books on networking.** Read the books that seem to make sense to you to build your skills and knowledge.

- **Talk to anyone and everyone possible** to get your message out and continue to gather marketplace information.

Understanding Relationship Networks

Although the concept of networking is occasionally maligned, the truth is, it is a very natural process that we do all the time in both our professional and our personal lives. Networking is simply talking with people and exchanging information about any number of topics from the mundane to the very serious. Most of us are involved in a number of different types of networks based on relationships.

The Definition of Relationship Networks

Relationship networks are comprised of people with whom we share certain interests, values or activities. For example, some relationship networks are made up of people with whom we currently work, others of people with whom we share a common religious, educational, professional or political affiliation, and still others with whom we share a neighborhood or community involvement.

In relationship networks, at least in the beginning, the information exchanged usually is based on our common interests or activities at the time. However, as relationships build over time, it is not uncommon to find that the topics of information discussed expand beyond the original shared foundation. For instance, you may find yourself talking to a long-time vendor about buying a new car or a former coworker about locating a good website for discount airline tickets.

Everyone you know and talk with is a member of your relationship network: relatives, friends, neighbors, former and current colleagues, vendors, other parents, other members of professional and community organizations, your doctor, your dentist, your CPA, your lawyer, and the list goes on.

The Benefits of Relationship Networking in Job Search

Talking with people to get your message out is an important part of job search. Conversations that are part of the normal maintenance of your relationship network are also ideally suited for gathering marketplace information and getting your career transition message out to others.

The members of your immediate relationship network, such as relatives, friends and close acquaintances, undoubtedly have an interest in talking with you. You already have a shared interest that easily can be expanded to conversations about organizations and mutual business matters. They also usually are willing to introduce you to people in their own relationship networks.

Relationship networking has value above and beyond finding new employment. It typically is used in career management by top performers who often get to the top in part because they have outstanding access to information through a business-related relationship network.

The following pages show some of the more important reasons for relationship networking or just plain talking to people in a job search.

 Productivity Pointer

Focus on Information, Not Openings

A common mistake in using relationship networks in search is focusing on job openings rather than getting information on target organizations. Your network contacts are unlikely to have information on openings, but may have information on one or more of your targets. Your best strategy is to establish contact with insiders at target organizations before the opening occurs.

Reasons for Relationship Networking

1. **Get your message out.**

   One important aspect of networking simply is getting your message out. The more people who know you are qualified and available, the better the chances that the information will get to the right person at the right time.

   The three most important components of getting your message out are your professional objective, your positioning statement (supported by target market information) and your exit statement. People who have this information – and also have been impressed by your interest and enthusiasm – are likely to help you spread the word. If you are conveying the right message, the more people who hear it, the better your chances are of connecting with a job. Effective job seekers find a way to work their basic message briefly into almost every conversation. It then spreads to various networks.

2. **Gather marketplace information.**

   The more information you gather on your target market, the more effective you are likely to be in your search. Who is doing what? What are the needs of various target organizations? What organizations are your kind of organization?

   It is important that you are well informed when you have networking conversations with people. When you tell someone that you have an interest in certain organizations, a logical question from them might be: *Really, why those organizations? What do you already know about them?* You do not want to seem unprepared or not to have any purpose behind your activities. Another important kind of information is the kind that allows you to do a reality check on your chosen career direction. This could include information on hiring practices, compensation levels and job descriptions. Do potential employers in your target market see you as a good candidate? Are there a large number of employers or just a few?

3. **Accumulate detailed information on your target organizations.**

   Research is vital to a well-executed job search. While a great deal of information can be gained from databases and reference books, your best source will be talking with people. As you prioritize your target list, you will want yo uncover specific information on your target companies, such as the names, interests, needs and personalities of the key people, the organizational culture, and how the companies get their work done. It also includes the organizational plans for the future and the names, addresses and telephone numbers of people inside the organization who might have more information.

   All of this information can be the subject of networking conversations that interest both parties. When you are networking with people employed in a certain industry, they usually are interested in other companies in the same industry. Their interest may be for competitive reasons, to help them do their job better, or because they know that some day they may be looking for new employment. Whatever their reasons, you can usually find significant common ground with people who are (or have been) employed in an industry you also know something about.

Reasons for Relationship Networking

4. **Get advice and ideas.**

   If you are talking to someone who is more experienced than you are, it may be appropriate for you to ask for career advice. Sometimes people enjoy mentoring someone less experienced. This kind of conversation could even lead someone to sponsor you in their own organization.

   In talking to someone on your own level, asking for career advice may create the impression that you are too unsure of yourself to be a good candidate. Asking for advice or ideas on your target market, however, can be very effective for everyone.

   Showing someone your list of target organizations and asking for their ideas and suggestions about which ones to pursue can be a very effective networking technique. It may produce target organizations you had not considered. It also may lead to conversations on specific organizations that enable you to collect detailed information. Properly handled, it also may result in introductions to people inside target organizations. All of these are useful in a job search. However, it is important to remember that when discussing target companies, you always must be clear that job openings or who is hiring are not your primary concerns.

5. **Locate sponsors or mentors.**

   Every now and then in the networking process, someone takes a particular liking to you. This may be personal in that the two of you are becoming friends. It may be professional in that your networking contact would like to see you join their organization in order to strengthen it. In either case, the person is prepared to promote you actively within their organization or to advise you on how to pursue employment there. Obviously, either of these options could be a major advantage. If you sense a person's willingness to become your sponsor, you might begin by asking for advice on how to best pursue their organization.

6. **Get referrals.**

   A very important potential benefit of networking is the possibility of getting referrals to people with whom you might begin new relationships. A referral is an introduction to a new contact, which increases the size of your relationship network and your chances of early success. Referrals also make new meetings easier to arrange. A stranger is more likely to be willing to meet with you if you have been recommended by a mutual acquaintance. So referrals are an important benefit of networking and also part of what makes relationship networking effective. Internet-based social networking sites offer excellent opportunities to make referral connections through your contacts.

Relationship Networking Adds to Your Entire Search Project

If you have done extensive relationship network building throughout your career transition, you will be able to:

- Be certain that your objective is realistic and obtainable.

- Know which organizations on your target list to pursue first.

- Present yourself in the interview as knowledgeable and interesting.

- Negotiate more effectively because you have insights on compensation practices in your chosen industry.

Compiling Your List of Networking Contacts

An obstacle some people in search face is believing that they do not know many people to contact. In actuality, your "Total Network" is bigger than you think. Your Total Network is all the people who will accept a phone call from you right now, without an introduction from a mutual acquaintance.

Our research shows that people usually estimate the size of their network between a half dozen and a couple hundred people. These numbers are way too small. Unless you've lived in a cave with someone bringing you food, your numbers are more than adequate.

The question is whether you're willing to take a hard look at all aspects of your personal network. The even bigger question is whether you're willing to make the effort to understand and effectively use that network to land a great new job.

Kinds of Network Connections

Your network connections can be divided into three categories: active, passive and dormant. Your active contacts are those people you speak to regularly. They are your friends, coworkers and fellow members of any organization. It could be your golfing buddy or your neighbor across the street.

If you know someone with whom you haven't spoken in more than a year, then that person falls into the dormant category. You could reactivate that dormant connection by getting back in touch and catching up on what's happening, if you feel so compelled.

Finally, there are the passive connections – those that have never been active. They are based on a common interest and could be activated. Any graduate of Yale, for example, has a connection to any other graduate, whether they have met or not.

Examining Your Network

Your Total Network is made up of numerous smaller networks. These smaller networks sometimes overlap, so that some people you know belong to several of your networks. Taking special note of these people could be useful because they might be even more inclined to assist in your search.

Now it's time to map your contacts. You may be surprised at all the names you can come up with. The exercise on the following page is designed to help you see who and where your contacts are. Having done that, you should look to see which of them are the best starting points for getting your message out and collecting marketplace information.

Tips and Techniques

The First 100 Contacts

A good starting point for general networking is to make a list of at least 100 possible contacts. Get out your current and past personal address books, business cards and email addresses and browse through them. Writing out a list is a useful exercise because it gets you thinking about all of your possible contacts. Include everyone who might take a call from you, even though you may not contact all of them.

Mapping Your Current Contact Network

Think about all of your contacts, whether they are active (you talk to them regularly), dormant (you used to talk to them) or passive (network connections that have not been activated). List a minimum of five contacts in each category. Then identify what type of contact that person is with an **"A"** for active, **"D"** for dormant or **"P"** for passive.

Friends, relatives, neighbors	Religious, alumni and professional organizations

Co-workers, suppliers, customers (past and present)	Personal business connections (banker, broker, CPA, lawyer, doctor, dentist)

Community, political groups	Your spouse's/partner's network

Understanding the Power of Networking

In order to get the word out and collect marketplace information, you need to talk with as many people as possible. The best place to start is also the easiest – your current circle of family members, friends and acquaintances. At the outset, just about anyone you are comfortable talking to is a good place to start.

Your task is to entice those people to talk to their friends and acquaintances about you. Then, hopefully, those people will talk about you to their contacts, and so on. This concept is akin to the "Six Degrees of Separation", also referred to as the "Human Web." In this long-standing theory which dates back to 1929, you can reach anyone on the planet through six steps.

In reality, job hunters usually succeed at the second and third degree of separation. Our experience tells us that you will probably go from a strong connection to one or two weaker ones to a job.

Suppose you start with a personal network of 10 people. Yours is probably much larger, but this is done for simplicity's sake. Now let's assume that those 10 people have a network of 10 people. Theoretically, you have now reached 100 people at the first and second degrees of separation.

From there, those 100 people know 10 people each, which means you are reaching 1,000 people at the third degree of separation. At the fourth degree, you have a staggering 10,000 people talking about you. It's doubtful you'll need anywhere near 10,000 people to succeed, but the number just grows from there.

This diagram shows two degrees of separation. If your network consisted of only 10 people, you would reach 100 people at the second degree.

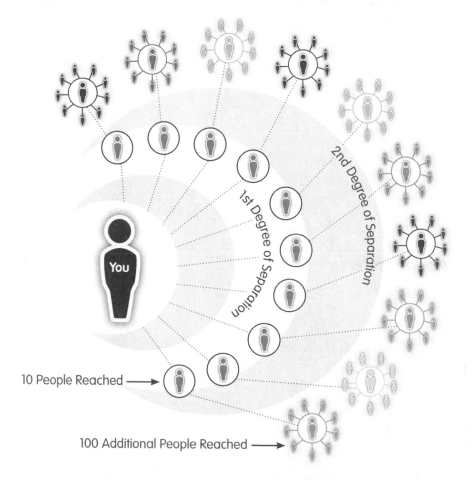

10 People Reached →

100 Additional People Reached →

Connecting with Your Networking Contacts

Once you have compiled your list of networking contacts, the question becomes: Where do you start? In getting your message out and gathering marketplace information, it is usually best to start with people you know well and are most comfortable talking to.

People in search sometimes feel that getting their message out with people they know well is not necessary. But take a closer look. If someone were to talk to a number of people who are close to you and concerned about you – your relatives, your golfing or shopping buddy, your best friend, your neighbors, your social acquaintances – how many of them would be clear about what it is that you do? How many of them would have any specifics on how well you do it?

For many of us, even people we are close to may not know the essential facts about our careers. Your neighbor's best friend could be desperate for candidates to fill a human resources position. But if your neighbor is unaware that you are an outstanding candidate for human resources manager, a valuable connection has been missed. Even if there is no open position at the moment, you should be talking to your neighbor's friend anyway, gathering information and getting referrals to other contacts. In order for people to assist you, they need information. And first degree contacts, when properly informed about you, your qualifications and exactly what you are looking for, will lead to second degree contacts. So it is important that you start by systematically talking with your immediate, first degree contacts.

Making the Initial Connection

Although you can do some of these early meetings on the phone, many times you might want to arrange a meeting to discuss your search. Many Lee Hecht Harrison candidates find that they get more information – even from friends and acquaintances – in person than on the phone, at least for the first conversation.

The following is a suggested dialogue for setting up a meeting.

Hello, Bill. This is Sam. I wanted to get together with you because I have recently left my position with ABS Company and would like to bounce some ideas off of you. Could we meet for a short discussion? I'd also like to show you the marketing plan I've put together for my search.

Start with Your Friends

Although job hunters are more likely to get connected to their next job through someone they know less well rather than through their close friends, friends are still the starting point. The final connection to your next employer will probably be through a weaker connection. So that friend of a friend of a friend may very well be the key to landing your dream job.

Be SMART in Conducting Network Meetings

The conversations you have with your contacts will combine getting your message out with gathering marketplace information. They also allow you to make use of your marketing plan and target list.

The SMART 5-Step Approach

Lee Hecht Harrison suggests a particular approach when meeting with your contacts: **SMART.** This approach is designed for use with your general network contacts such as the ones you identified earlier in this chapter. When you are able to talk to people inside your target companies, you will want to switch to the **SELL** approach, which is discussed in Milestone 7.

The SMART meeting includes:

S	M	A	R	T
Summarize Your Message	**Marketing Plan**	**Ask Questions**	**Referrals**	**Trade Information**
Use your professional objective, positioning statement and, if necessary, your exit statement.	Describe your marketing plan and provide a copy of your target list.	Ask about organizations on your target list and their issues, strengths, problems and people.	Always ask for introductions to others who might have more information on the organizations you discussed. And ask for introductions to target company insiders, including hiring managers, when possible.	Always try to give your conversational partner useful information. Make the conversation a two-way street whenever possible.

Agenda for Meeting with Contacts

The SMART approach provides an agenda for meeting with your general networking contacts. Allow approximately 20 to 30 minutes for a meeting. We have included suggested time allowances.

1. **Summarize your message (2 minutes)** Start with your professional objective and positioning statement; use your exit statement if needed. These will give your contact the basic information. Describe your professional objective, giving two or three examples of positions typical of that objective. State why you believe you are qualified, mentioning your competencies. Use your accomplishment statements to back up your claims. They contain all the information the person needs to understand you and how they can help. Be brief and summarize. You scheduled the meeting to obtain information, not sell your qualifications. So give only the information that is needed in order to prepare the person for the rest of the conversation.

2. **Marketing plan (3–4 minutes)** Introduce the key elements of your marketing plan. You already have mentioned your professional objective, so move to a description of your targeted industries and your geographical and organizational size preferences, and explain why you have made these decisions. Introduce the list of targeted companies that meet your criteria.

3. **Ask questions (10–15 minutes)** Move from identifying target companies to asking questions about them and discussing each category. Listen carefully and take notes when appropriate. Prior to the meeting, make a list of questions you want to ask in order to direct the conversation and collect information about target organizations, including the names of any relevant inside contacts. Use open-ended questions to encourage your contact to share information. In a similar manner, discussions of issues in your field or industry also may lead to the names of relevant people.

4. **Referrals (3–6 minutes)** Once you have asked questions and gathered information, you may specifically request referrals. This is easier if your contact has already mentioned names. You can now repeat some of those names and ask for an introduction. If no names have been mentioned, ask if your contact knows people who might have more information or the names of people inside any of your target organizations. Be sure to get specific names and titles and confirm how and when you will approach the referrals. Ideally, try to get your contact to make the preliminary contact for you. If your contact cannot think of any people for you to see, ask if you can call back in a few days to see if any have come to mind.

5. **Trade information (2-3 minutes)** You come to this meeting with useful information, whether you realize it or not. Be on the alert for opportunities to trade the information with your contact. You may know about...

   - the industry
   - solutions other organizations have found to problems mentioned by your contact
   - other organizations
   - names of potential candidates the company may want to recruit (other than yourself)
   - contacts with professional groups, suppliers and other resources

   The chance to trade information might come. Keep in mind: *What do I know that might be useful to this contact?* You also may offer to introduce your contact to others.

6. **Closing the Meeting** Once you have started your network meeting, keep in mind any time agreement. If you stay beyond the agreed upon time, your contact may allow it out of courtesy, but may feel less inclined to give you referrals. Arrange any necessary follow up. Explain that you will inform your contact of what happens in the referral meetings. Conclude the meeting with your thanks.

SAMPLE

SMART Script

Opening

Introduce yourself and mention who referred you.

Kyle Johnson of Sanchez Health Systems suggested I contact you. Kyle and I went to State University together, and he suggested you might be someone I could speak to about pharmaceutical and chemical firms in the New Jersey area.

Summarize Your Message

As a result of the acquisition of Sherman Corporation, my position as an environmental health and safety manager was eliminated. I have particular strengths in management, auditing, remediation and training. I am now looking for a new position in that field or the related areas of compliance auditing or regulatory affairs. I think I am a strong candidate for both management and consulting positions in the field because …

Marketing Plan

As you can see from my marketing plan, I am conducting my search primarily in New York, New Jersey and Connecticut. I consider chemical and pharmaceutical companies with more than 1,000 employees to be my most likely targets. I am also pursuing consulting firms of any size. You'll notice that I have a list of organizations fitting my size and location criteria in each of the three industry categories.

Ask Questions

- *Which of those categories are you most familiar with?*
- *Which companies are you familiar with in that category? What do you know about them?*
- *Do you know of any that have strong environmental health or safety concerns?*
- *Have you ever used an environmental, health and safety consulting firm?*
- *Do you know anyone who might have?*
- *Can you think of any other organizations that should be on my list?*

- *Are you familiar with the _____ industry?*
- *What do you know about …?*
- *How would I find out more about that?*
- *Do you know who is in charge of that?*
- *Do you know someone who might know more?*
- *What are the biggest issues they are facing right now?*
- *What is your opinion of …?*
- *Can you tell me how that company is structured?*

Referrals

You mentioned that you knew a couple of people at Amalgamated Pharmaceuticals and someone at Hazmat Consulting. These are exactly the kind of people I want to talk to. I want to find out more about who is doing what in environmental health and safety. Would you be willing to introduce me to them?

Trade Information

I'll send you the article we discussed on career management during M&A situations, and I'll get you Sarah's phone number. I think you'll really enjoy hearing what she has to say about your competitors and their sales plans.

Closing

I really appreciate your offering to introduce me to Gail Whitestone-Smith, Thomas Lee and Gary Jacobs. Would you be willing to email them so they'll be expecting my call? I'll let you know how the meetings go.

Building and Maintaining a Strong Network

After a SMART meeting, send an email or letter to your contact within 24 hours. Make sure you follow up with any promised actions in a timely manner. Generally, an email will suffice in this instance. If your meeting was with a knowledgeable contact whom you did not know well, you could send a typed letter.

Contacts who have been particularly helpful to you should be contacted once every two-to-four weeks during your search. Contacts can be by phone (best) or an email. Some people cut out articles that would be of interest to a network contact and drop them in the mail with a short note such as:

> Dave
> – Saw this article and thought you
> might be interested. Laura

For all others, consider reconnecting with them during the search to let them know your status or to pass along information you think might be of interest to them.

Reach Out to Target Company Insiders

Begin to build new relationships by reaching out from your initial first degree contacts to people you have not met. Beyond gathering marketplace information and getting your message out, the objective is, of course, to meet with insiders at target companies and, eventually, get through to the hiring manager.

Throughout your job search, you want to expand your network of contacts. Not only will this get your message out to more people and accelerate your search, it also will give you the benefit of a larger relationship network after you start a new position.

Contact Referrals

As your search expands to new contacts you have been referred to, you will need to pay more attention to setting up meetings. Initial contacts will talk to you because they already know you. Your most powerful opening with those who do not know you is a referral and introduction. You also may mention that you have information they might be interested in.

Preparation is important when contacting a referral who does not know you. First, be clear on your objective. You are gathering marketplace information and ideas – and you have some to share as well.

Always begin with the referral's name when introducing yourself:

> Hello Ms. DeMario, I am calling you at the suggestion of Kimberly Olson. She suggested that you would be a good source of information on …

Next, get right to the point, the meeting:

> Ms. DeMario, I would like to stop by your office to meet with you for 15 or 20 minutes to get your reaction to information on the financial services industry that I have collected as part of my current career transition. Ms. Olson said you were very knowledgeable on financial services in Los Angeles and thought that you would be the ideal person to speak to. Would Wednesday be a good day for you, or would next week be better?

Since your objective on this initial phone call is to set up a meeting, not to conduct the meeting, say only as much as is needed to do that. Sometimes a note or email before the phone call helps. The best method is always to have your initial contact mention you to the second degree contact before you call.

Keep your initial networking contacts informed of your subsequent meeting with referrals.

Climbing "The Ladder" of Networking Contacts

The ultimate professional contact is the hiring manager, the person who could be your next boss. You'll probably have to work your way up to that person. This can be related to climbing a ladder. At the bottom are personal contacts, community members and good friends. At the top are the hiring managers you have never met. Step-by-step, you look for ways to move up and get into that right job in the right organization. You are always looking for ways to get introduced to people higher on the ladder.

A key point to know is that you must treat your professional contacts differently from your personal contacts. Follow these guidelines:

- **Be more cautious about asking for favors.**

- **Offer information as well as asking for it.**

- **Don't use your Target List with insiders.**

- **Be judicious about asking for referrals.**

- **Your conversations should be more businesslike.**

At the bottom of your personal contacts' ladder is your Inner Circle, which includes all the people you know best. They are your friends, acquaintances and relatives. Your Middle Circle includes community relationships and those people with whom you are not as close. Your Outer Circle include dormant personal relationships such as your former college classmates. All of these personal contacts are considered to be one degree of separation from you.

Your ladder of professional contacts includes three levels: At the bottom is Level Three, which includes professional contacts who are not in the same line of work as you are.

Level Two includes people you know who work inside your targets, below your level or in departments you're not interested in. Then there is your ultimate goal – Level One. It includes your potential next boss, your boss's boss and anyone higher. It also includes Influencers – anyone who has your boss's ear whom he trusts.

You could be lucky enough to jump straight from a personal friend to the hiring manager. If you find yourself in that extraordinary case, make sure you are prepared or delay making the contact until you are.

The next milestone will prepare you for your conversation with the hiring manager, whether you made the giant leap to the top of "The Ladder" or the slow climb.

The Ladder of Networking Contacts

Start at the bottom and work your way up. Whenever you use your Target List, look for the opportunity to get introduced to new people.

Professional Contacts

Level One
Hiring Managers and influencers

Do not use your Target List

Level Two
Insiders and professional peers

Use your Target List with professional peers, but not with insiders

Level Three
All other work-related contacts

Use your Target List or mention some targets

Personal Contacts

Outer Circle
Dormant Contacts:
Former inner or middle, but no recent contact

Passive Contacts:
You have an organizational or community connection, but never met this particular person

When appropriate, use your Target List or mention some targets

Middle Circle
Community and organizational contacts whom you have met

Use your Target List or mention some targets

Inner Circle
Friends, acquaintances and relatives; people you talk to regularly

Always use your Target List

This chart is from *Highly Effective Networking: Meet the Right People and Get a Great Job*, by Orville Pierson. Used with permission.

SAMPLE Networking Emails

Dealing with Unfamiliar Contacts

INITIAL CONTACT:

To: Jason Jones
From: Alan Hertzig (hertzig@example.com)
Re: Referred by Patricia Hart

Patricia Hart suggested that you would be a good resource for me to speak with. I have been collecting information on new approaches to marketing in healthcare as part of my current career transition. Pat said you are very knowledgeable in this area.

I would like to stop by your office to show you what I have learned so far and see if you might have additional information. I will call next week to see what time would be good for you.

After what Pat told me, I'm very much looking forward to meeting you.

Regards,
Alan Hertzig

FOLLOW-UP CONTACT:

To: Jason Jones
From: Alan Hertzig (hertzig@example.com)
Re: Follow-up to our meeting

Thank you for taking the time to meet with me last Tuesday. Just by way of update, I already have contacted Bernadette Vanek and Mark Clifford and made appointments. I will continue to keep you posted.

Attached is information on the two consultants we discussed. I hope they are able to assist you with your project.

Regards,
Alan Hertzig

Advantages of Using the Internet for Networking

1. **Expands your circle of contacts and helps you locate that hiring manager or next great opportunity.**

2. **Does not involve a telephone call or a personal meeting. This tends to eliminate most of the fear of the first meeting.**

3. **Does not require an introduction from a primary contact on your list.**

4. **Often offers immediate results.**

5. **Simplifies your record keeping by using an electronic address book.**

Using the Power of Social Media

Networking online combines traditional networking with the power of the Internet. It allows you to create a community of virtual contacts who can provide information on job leads, industry trends and possible openings. As enticing as networking online can be, remember that nothing is more effective than meeting a hiring manager face to face. Your goal – whatever method you use to contact people initially – is to get the opportunity to meet the hiring manager in person.

Social Media Websites

Most social media sites were set up with the goal of people making personal connections. MySpace and other similar sites were originally used as a means for the youth to express themselves and communicate. But the number of sites soon exploded, and the whole idea expanded to the adult generations. It also has expanded in the area of job search.

Now more than 600 million registered users around the world are connected on Facebook. LinkedIn quickly took over the area of expertise in the professional sector. Twitter is all about microblogging, both personal and professional. And other sites took over their own niches. Within this massive social networking Web, there exists a whole lot of networking potential.

What You Need to Do

Get yourself out there. Start by setting up a social media profile on LinkedIn. Build your professional brand through this free marketing tool. Showcase your talents.

Also make connections through Facebook and other social media sites, if you so choose.

While you're connecting with your friends and colleagues, however, beware of any incriminating messages or photos that you may be putting out there for the world to see.

Most corporate recruiters and hiring managers are realizing the power of social media and are turning to the Web to source and screen their candidates. When you get past the virtual process and into their office for an interview, you might be amazed at how much they already know about you.

Google Yourself

It's a good idea to Google yourself. See what employers can discover about you instantly. Your presence out there might surprise you.

Do a simple search of your name in the Google search engine. You also might try variations of your name, such as including your middle initial. Among other things, your LinkedIn profile automatically will pop up – making it even more important that you are represented with an updated LinkedIn profile.

And don't miss the Google images link. Floating around in cyberspace might be some incriminating photos of you – or perhaps just an amusing pose of you from 10 years ago.

Setting Boundaries

It's smart to utilize the privacy settings that certain social media websites offer. For example, Facebook lets you customize who gets to see your photos, your bio, your status, your religious affiliation, your political views and more. Whether you choose to let just your friends, friends of friends, or everyone see your information is up to you.

By law, things such as your religious affiliation or other personal information should not prevent an employer from hiring you. But you may not want to take that chance. Even if you have a handicap, or have had a long-term illness that kept you out of work – discussing it on your social network might not be wise.

In short, take control of your presence on the Internet, and then use its power to work for you.

The New Age of Networking

t's all about going mobile. Job seekers and employers alike are tuned in online almost 24/7 connecting with others. Whether they're on the computer, iPad, tablet, iPhone or other Smart phone, it's all about communication.

In this busy, fast-paced world, true face time is at a premium. To earn those coveted few minutes for an actual meeting, you have to be out there connecting by whatever means possible.

LinkedIn Apps

By now, you should have your profile on LinkedIn at the very least. LinkedIn has iPhone and Android apps as well as an HTML5 mobile website to keep you totally connected to a community of virtual contacts who can provide information on job leads, industry trends and job openings.

Consider Branchout and Others

Beyond LinkedIn, you have to figure out the sites that work best for you and your career path. Google+, for instance, offers the most potential for those in IT, engineering and other technical fields.

Facebook is fast becoming a powerhouse in the job hunting area. Two Facebook apps, Branchout and Monster's networking app BeKnown, allow Facebook users to isolate their professional networking efforts and contacts within Facebook while leveraging a person's Facebook network information.

Glassdoor is offering Inside Connections" which uses Facebook to uncover whom your friends know at a company that could help land you a job.

Get on the TweetDeck, in the HootSuite

Twitter is a good way to research news on a company. There are Twitter tools such as TweetDeck and HootSuite to manage a user's feeds, lists contacts.

All this technological advancement has certainly broken down many barriers as job seekers network to find new jobs. But to be truly effective online, you need to organize your network contacts, learn to make the important first contacts, engage your existing network, then grow and expand your network using social media sites.

As more social networking apps continue to hit the market, realize these are powerful tools – use them wisely and protect your online brand.

Using Job Boards of All Sizes

Their names have become part of our vernacular — Monster, CareerBuilder, TheLadders, Dice, SimplyHired, Indeed. Job boards are all over the Internet — but not just the big boards. There are tens of thousands of big and small boards vying for attention.

For active managerial and professional hunters, the large boards are not always the best. Often, it's a niche board specializing in a profession, industry, salary level or location important to the job hunter that's most useful. A specialty board such as ComputerWork.com or GreenJobSearch.org also might prove more effective.

Don't Forget Company Job Boards

According to an analysis of hiring data by Jobs2web Inc., companies look through about 219 applications from a large job board before making one hire as compared to 33 applications per hire on the company's own site.

For job hunters, the biggest negative of job boards is that they can take an inordinate amount of time — much more time than is justified by the likely results. It takes time to locate them, time to list on them and time to track anything they come up with. And they sometimes generate a lot of spam, including offers of high-priced job search assistance services, some of which have proven to be of very little use.

The Downside to Job Boards

Like any commercial website, job boards often seek advertising revenue, so they work hard to keep users on the site, reading job hunting advice and other content. Sometimes that advice is offered by bona fide experts. Sometimes it's not. It's usually produced by multiple authors, and therefore can lack coherence.

The other big problem is that perhaps thousands of other job seekers are seeing that same posting and applying just like you. There is a good likelihood that your resume ends up in a huge pile on a human resource person's desk. You may have an outstanding resume — and included all the key words to get their attention. But it still may never see the light of day in a hiring manager's office. The odds are not in your favor.

So, Should a Job Hunter Use Job Boards?

Yes. Will those job boards produce results? Yes, for some people, but probably to just a small portion. Especially during difficult economic times, jobs tend to change hands by informal means. This makes basic networking even more important.

The bottom line: Limit the amount of time spent on job boards.

Tips and Techniques

Repost often
You should update your posted resume on a regular basis, if only to change a word or two and repost. Many job boards allow employers to search only the newest resumes or those posted within the last few weeks or months. So, reposting your resume increases your chances of its being found.

Think local
In addition to visiting all the top job sites, job seekers should utilize local sites that cover their city or state. Use the jobs by state directory to find job opening in your location. Websites for your Local Chambers of Commerce and local online newspapers are good resources for identifying companies to apply.

Search LHH's JobScout
Take advantage of the job board on the CRN. JobScout, powered by SimplyHired, gives you access to millions of job openings that are being posted on job boards and company websites. This is exclusive to LHH candidates.

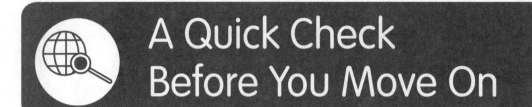

A Quick Check Before You Move On

Getting Your Message Out is where your marketing effort (and all the work you've done on it) begins to take flight. It's really at the heart of your job search effort.

Before you leave this milestone:

Go to Career Resource Network (CRN) to find:

- Tips on how to post your resume, manage your Internet presence, and build your brand

- Samples of letters and email messages you can use for networking, both for getting the initial meeting and following up after it

- More on the SMART method – with timed agendas and scripts

- Downloadable e-learning and podcasts to help you sharpen your skills

Get in the habit of using email to secure meetings and to update your network contacts from time to time. You don't want to be bothersome, but you do want to maintain awareness of your search among people who can help you. And make sure you have a professional-sounding, business-appropriate email address.

Milestone 7

Talk With Hiring Managers

Why this Milestone is Important...

Talking with hiring managers is the single most important activity in a search. Setting up and having successful meetings with hiring managers has been the focus of your search activities up to this point for a very simple reason: when the right job comes along, it will be a hiring manager who makes the decision to hire you.

How you get to talk with hiring managers does not matter. Some people in search are very successful in setting up meetings with hiring managers through recruiters, ads or online job banks. For others, these methods are less successful or do not work at all. Referrals to hiring managers are the single most common way of getting in to see them, but they are often difficult to get. Whichever way you do it, talking with hiring managers is essential.

Talking with Hiring Managers
Before There Is an Opening Raises Your Odds

Most people in job search succeed by talking with hiring managers before those managers have a need. Once there is an opening, the competition can be intense. People who have been able to establish contact with a hiring manager before an opening often find the communication easier and are frequently able to circumvent a complex hiring process completely. Talking with hiring managers in your chosen target companies before there is a need for your services raises the odds that at least one of them will have a need within a reasonable period of time. Being in the right place at the right time is not an accident. It is the result of methodically working a good marketing plan.

Talking with More Hiring Managers
Reduces Your Search Time

Lee Hecht Harrison research conducted since 1992 shows that a typical candidate talks to a total of between 20 and 30 appropriate hiring managers before concluding an employment arrangement with one of those managers. In a very strong job market, the average number of conversations with hiring managers may be less than 20; in a poor job market, the average may be more than 30. However, the range of 20 to 30 has held fairly steady over the years.

Lee Hecht Harrison candidates typically have an average of two conversations a week with hiring managers. There is a clear correlation between the frequency of these conversations and the length of a search. Those candidates with shorter searches talk with 50% more hiring managers each week (2.7 versus 1.8) than those with longer searches.

It is important to note that these numbers are averages. Some lucky people are hired by the first hiring manager they talk with, whereas others, with less luck or more difficult searches in more difficult markets, may talk with many more than 30.

How Many Hiring Managers
Will You Need to Talk With?

There are a number of reasons why some people in search talk with a large number of hiring managers and others succeed by talking only to a small number. Some of the reasons include luck and the difficulty of the search. There are also more controllable factors, such as the quality of your marketing plan, the effectiveness of your communications strategy, your skill in meeting people and collecting information and any personal barriers you may have, such as procrastination.

Gauging Your Success

The difficulty of the search can be estimated after the marketing plan is completed. For nearly everyone, Milestone 5, Gather Marketplace Information, is an important part of gauging the difficulty of the planned search. How do knowledgeable people react to your qualifications and marketing plan? Do people inside of your chosen target companies say that you are the kind of person typically hired by their companies? Or do they suggest that you are in some way a marginal candidate?

Why this Milestone is Important...

Paying attention to these early signs is an important part of gauging the difficulty of a search and the total number of hiring managers that you will need to talk with.

Selling Yourself to the Hiring Manager

Initial conversations with hiring managers, especially when there is no opening, tend to be informal. There is less pressure and a hiring manager is much less likely to ask you the same types of questions you would expect in a formal interview. However, all conversations with hiring managers, regardless of how casual they may be, are a form of an interview and require more initiative and skill on your part to guide the conversation.

Lee Hecht Harrison recommends a particular approach to meetings with hiring managers called SELL. Basically, the approach involves taking a consultative selling approach. Unlike the more direct sales approach a used-car salesperson might take, this approach tries to elicit the needs of the customer (the hiring manager) and suggest how your product (you) might meet those needs. The intent of this type of selling is to establish a long-term, more trusting relationship – a relationship that might be the key to your future employment.

People Who Talk With More Hiring Managers Each Week Have Shorter Searches

A study of Lee Hecht Harrison candidates resulted in the following findings:

Length of Search	Average Number of Conversations with Hiring Managers (per week)
Top Quarter (those with the shortest searches)	**2.7**
Second Quarter	**2.2**
Third Quarter	**2.2**
Bottom Quarter (those with the longest searches)	**1.8**

Questions to Explore

- *Do I know any hiring managers at my target companies?*

- *How can I meet peers in my target organizations who might give me information about a hiring manager or who might introduce me to one?*

- *Am I listed on a social networking site? How can I leverage this resource?*

- *Have I gathered enough marketplace information about my target companies to anticipate some of their needs and to demonstrate how I can address those needs?*

- *What will I say when I talk with the hiring manager in each of my target organizations?*

- *Do I have a list of questions to ask in interviews that will enable me to gather the information I need?*

Suggested Actions

- **Share your target list with colleagues and friends** and ask for names of insiders at target companies, particularly hiring managers.

- **If your networking activities are not generating enough names of hiring managers, try other approaches:**
  - Examine company profiles, articles and databases to get names.
  - Call the target companies and ask for the name of the appropriate manager.

- **Be prepared for SELL meetings by researching the organization thoroughly.**

Connecting with Hiring Managers

Sooner or later, your Level Three and Two networking conversations will produce introductions to Level One contacts, the hiring manager – especially if you remember to ask for them. Your lower-level contact could instantly become a hero for producing a great job candidate and saving the company money in headhunter fees and prolonged candidate searches.

Meanwhile, you have to thoroughly research the hiring manager. You need to know that person's official title at the company. Check the Internet for background information. Talk to your networking partners and map the hiring manager's networks. Look for common interests because the more you find, the more possible conversation topics you have. If you "hit it off," you're ahead of the game.

Setting up the meeting

The single best way to get through to a hiring manager and set up a meeting is to have an introduction from a mutual acquaintance. If that person is willling to call or email the hiring manager before you do, setting an appointment might be very easy. With no introduction, you'll just have to work a little harder.

Generally, your objective is to make the appointment and get off the phone. A personal meeting is to your advantage – don't let a long phone conversation turn into a substitute for that. Be prepared, however, if your contact insists on it. That means having your exit statement, positioning statement and resume in front of you. And, of course, you've already done your research on the company.

Expressing a genuine informed interest can overcome a weak resume. Make sure you know enough to be believable. An interested, enthusiastic candidate is highly appealing to hiring managers. A highly-skilled person who is not very interested may not be productive and easily could quit. A highly interested person is likely to get more skilled with every passing day.

Also, always remember the hiring manager's agenda. The higher up that person is, the less time on the schedule for you. The hiring manager is thinking four basic things:

1. **What's in it for me?**

2. **What do you want from me?**

3. **Is this going to be awkward or difficult?**

4. **How long will it take and will it be worth that amount of time?**

It's up to you to prove that you're worth the effort.

Productivity Pointer

All meetings with hiring managers (in person or on the phone) should be treated as interviews, and your preparation should be thorough. (As part of your preparation, you may want to read the chapter for Milestone 9.)

Structure of the Call

- **Open the conversation by introducing yourself and explaining why you are calling.** If you were referred by a mutual acquaintance, mention that person's name immediately.

  My name is Brittany Jordan. Frank Gomez suggested I give you a call because of my background as a field sales manager in our industry.

- **Provide a reason for a meeting,** suggesting some value for the hiring manager. The value may simply be your background and experience, or it may be more specific.

  Frank and I worked together at Namebrand Pharmaceuticals. I'm relocating to the East Coast and would like to get your thoughts on the various players in the industry in New Jersey. As part of my preparation for relocating, I have done considerable research on key industry issues and trends, which you may find interesting.

- **Suggest a meeting time.**

  I'd like to stop by your office and get acquainted. Would morning or afternoon work better for you?

 Calls to Hiring Managers

- *This is Gail Jackson. I understand that you manage the engineering group that developed the XYZ product. I talked to one of your engineering team leaders, Anthony Lazzaro, last week, and he said that your project is going to accelerate your move to the top of the industry. I'm an engineer with 10 years of experience in our industry. In fact, I managed a very similar project at ABC Company and have been researching the latest technology. I am very interested in discussing this with you. Would next week be possible?*

- *My name is Dawn Davis. I heard your speech at the conference last week. I'm a human resources professional with special expertise in mergers and acquisitions. I have worked with very diverse populations – from shop superintendents to senior executives. Your remarks kindled some thoughts for me that I think might be relevant to your company's current situation. I'd like to share them with you. I'll be in town the latter part of next week. Can we set up an appointment for next Thursday or Friday?*

- *This is Kevin Chang. I just finished reading an article about your company in yesterday's Times. As a senior banker who has started up new branches and turned around poor-performing operations, I really connected with some of the challenges your company is facing, particularly your new affiliate here in Seattle. If you have the time and interest, I think you might like to hear about some of the methods I've used over the years. I could come by sometime next week. Would you have 20 or 30 minutes to meet with me then?*

Why Will a Hiring Manager Talk to You?

Whether you have an introduction or not, you should ask yourself why a particular hiring manager might be willing to take the time to talk to you. The answers to this question usually fall into one of four categories:

INFORMATION
You have information that might be helpful to the hiring manager.

- The marketplace information you have been gathering as part of your work in Milestone 5 can pay big dividends here.

- You are much better informed than most people you will be meeting with on industries, organizations within them and their activities.

- In this age of abundant information, people need and depend on accurate and up-to-date information to help them be effective in their professional and personal lives.

- Unfortunately, most of us are often too busy to conduct and organize the research we need.

- As someone who has been immersed in the latest information, you represent a valuable resource to hiring managers.

COMMON INTERESTS
You and the hiring manager share a common interest, work-related or not.

- This is actually a way of focusing your information gathering.

- Your contacts might appreciate information on golf, shopping, cars or child care as much as they appreciate work-related information.

IDEAS
You have well-thought-out ideas that might help the hiring manager in some way.

- Again, this goes back to information gathering and common interests.

- Your ideas must be related to real world facts and of interest to your listener.

- When they are, a phone call from you can be a pleasure rather than a nuisance.

UNANNOUNCED STAFFING NEEDS
The hiring manager is quietly looking for a new employee.

- Sometimes a chance to evaluate a possible new employee without admitting they are doing so is attractive to hiring managers.

- People who are looking to hire would often prefer to avoid the problems and expense of hiring recruiters and placing ads and Internet postings.

Meeting with Hiring Managers

Although you might think of the meetings you have with insiders, especially with hiring managers, at your target organizations as networking opportunities, they are very different from general networking SMART meetings. Meetings with hiring managers, even when there is no known opening, need to be thought of as pre-interview meetings, because sooner or later the organization will have a need and you need to position yourself as a prime candidate.

The SELL 4-Step Approach

Lee Hecht Harrison recommends a particular approach when meeting with hiring managers: **SELL.** This approach is designed for use with contacts inside target organizations, especially hiring managers and those above that level. It is more focused than the SMART approach discussed in Milestone 6, and does not include the use of a marketing plan or target list.

S	**E**	**L**	**L**
Summarize Your Message	**Explore Their Needs**	**Link Your Benefits to Their Needs**	**Leverage a Next Contact**
Use your professional objective, positioning statement and, if necessary, your exit statement.	Collecting further information about the needs of the targeted organization and of this particular hiring manager is central to this discussion. This information will enable you to be even more effective in your continuing pursuit of the organization, both in this meeting and after it.	To the degree possible, mention the competencies you have that might fit the needs of the organization.	Use information obtained in this meeting to arrange a next contact.

Agenda for Meeting with Hiring Managers

The SELL approach actually provides you with an agenda for meeting with hiring managers. Assuming the meeting to be 20 to 30 minutes in length, we have included a suggested time allowance for each segment.

1. **Summarize your message (3 minutes)**

   Use your professional objective, your positioning statement and, if necessary, your exit statement. Your initial message about yourself should position you as someone who would be an asset to any organization, but with special emphasis on any competencies or accomplishments that are relevant to the needs of this particular organization, based on what you have learned. This may mean modifying your positioning statement. For example, Grisele, a technical writer, had targeted certain companies that had internal marketing departments and did not normally hire technical writers. With these organizations, Grisele repositioned her introduction by saying:

   I help companies support their products in a form customers can understand.

   This puts the attention on the value of what she did in a way that these organizations can relate to it.

2. **Explore their needs (10 – 15 minutes)**

   As an old saying goes: There are those who listen and those who wait to talk. Keep this in mind when exploring needs with hiring managers. Your research and analysis of the organization may have led you to conclude that your skills and experience match their needs. However, before you try to convince the hiring manager of that, you should be sure you correctly understand all of the needs – as well as the hiring manager's perspective on them. You should prepare relevant questions in advance and ask them early in the meeting. And then, you must listen. Listening is the way you will get the information you need to recommend yourself as the solution for their needs. Smile, nod, stay focused and let the person know you are hearing what they are saying. Interject phrases, such as:

   Oh, I've heard that. Yes, I agree. That's interesting.

   Summarize what you believe are the main points presented by the hiring manager. Ask for confirmation that you understood correctly. Above all, listen and connect. Do what you can to build a relationship.

3. **Link your benefits to their needs (5 – 10 minutes)**

   After you have a better picture of the organization's or hiring manager's needs, you can better describe yourself as relevant to those needs. Now is the time to embellish the brief summary you used at the outset. Select those competencies and accomplishments that clearly connect to the needs you confirmed. In your responses, reflect back some of the actual words the hiring manager used. This is where the research you have done and the information you are getting from the hiring manager come together. This is when you begin to link your experience and skills to the needs that are being expressed.

4. **Leverage a next contact (2 minutes)**

   Building relationships with hiring managers is one of the most effective ways to be sure you are in their thoughts when an opening does occur. For this reason, you want to leverage a next contact with a hiring manager, or at least find a way to continue the conversation. Throughout the meeting, you have been looking for shared interests that might give you a reason for another meeting or a follow-up contact. One way to do this is making an offer of additional information on a topic of interest, after you have had time to collect it. If possible, make a specific appointment for another meeting, for a specific length of time. If you are not able to arrange a meeting on the spot, continue contact by following up with the hiring manager in whatever ways seem appropriate. At the very end, leave your resume with the hiring manager.

SELL Script

Opening

I read your article in last week's Technology Today, and Eileen Williams suggested we might get acquainted. Eileen and I were colleagues at ABC Corporation several years ago. I understand from Eileen that you head up the Technology Division. Is that correct?

Summarize Your Message

I'm an Information Technology Manager with a background in the application of technology in the areas of marketing, sales, manufacturing and accounting. I have worked with a Fortune 500 company very similar to yours and have run my own business as a consultant to large firms in the IS/IT areas. I have extensive experience in accounting applications.

Explore Their Needs

- *Based on what you said in your article, it sounds as if you are encountering some real challenges in integrating accounting applications across the enterprise. Is that correct? Can you tell me more about that?*
- *I read that your company recently introduced EntreWizard software. How is that working out?*
- *What are your goals for your area of responsibility for the next year?*
- *What do you see as the greatest recent contributions of your department to the firm as a whole?*
- *What are some of your biggest challenges?*
- *What kinds of projects are you engaged in now?*
- *What do you see as the most important qualities in an IT manager?*

Link Your Benefits to Their Needs

As a consultant and an internal IT person, I've taken many of the same approaches as you have with accounting applications. I once had a situation similar to the one you described with your Peoria unit. In that case, I …

When I introduced EntreWizard at United Amalgamated, we were faced with some sticky problems with certain users …

I certainly can identify with those last two challenges you mentioned. My experience …

Leverage a Next Contact

My research on EntreWizard certainly tracks with your experience. I expect to talk to other large users in the next few weeks. If I discover anything that might apply to your situation, I'll give you a call.

I know a consultant who often works with accounting applications of exactly the type you described. He may have some contacts among the programmers who created them. Sometimes they can provide information more useful than what you get through normal channels. I'll ask him if he can provide any introductions and get back to you. Would next Tuesday be a good time to call you?

CLOSING

Based on what I knew before I came today, I liked your organization. I'm leaving with even more admiration for what you're doing here. It also looks like you and I might have some shared interests, especially in the applications area. I'd really like to stay in touch. I'll call you next Tuesday and let you know what I found out about the programmers.

SMART vs. SELL: How They Differ

In Milestone 6, we discussed using the SMART approach in networking meetings. You will recall that with SMART, you summarize your message, describe your marketing plan, ask questions, ask for referrals and trade information. There are some fundamental differences between the SMART and the SELL approach, as shown in the chart below:

SMART	SELL
• Meetings with people not currently employed at your target organizations.	• Meetings with people inside target organizations, at your level and higher, especially hiring managers.
• Early networking meetings designed to gather information and get your message out broadly.	• Serious conversations with insiders at targets designed to cultivate an interest in you.
• Job leads are not expected, but may occur.	• It is only a matter of time until this organization has an appropriate opening; treat every conversation like an interview.
• Always ask for referrals.	• Do not ask for referrals because this may convey a lack of interest in this organization.
• Pay attention to continuing or building the relationship.	• Build as many working relationships as possible – one day you may be working there.

Tips and Techniques

Working with Gatekeepers

- Treat every gatekeeper with courtesy and respect.
- Identify yourself. If you do not, you are likely to encounter resistance, especially if you ask immediately for information.
- Enlist the gatekeeper's help in getting you through to the person you want. They know procedures, schedules and the best way to reach someone.
- Make a note of the person's name. Use it in conversation and when you call the next time.
- Try the following when introducing yourself to a gatekeeper:

    Hello, my name is Anna Sing. Jim Taylor suggested I talk with Steve Gleason.
    Is he still the director of human resources?

- Voicemail is also a gatekeeper you will encounter. Leave a brief message explaining why you are calling, who referred you and when you will call back.

Following Up with Hiring Managers

Take a deep breath. You're not done yet. One of the most important things you'll do in job search is follow-up. Even if you're not seeing any encouraging signs, stay with it. Keep on telling them how interested you are.

Once you have talked to an appropriate hiring manager, you should recontact that person every two or three weeks until they hire you – or another company does. How often you make contact depends on how highly paid the job is. Higher-paying jobs require contact every three weeks. In lower paying jobs, make contact more often.

Lee Hecht Harrison did a study on this and found that the most effective job hunters - the ones who get jobs more quickly – did a great deal more follow-up with hiring managers. It clearly showed that those job hunters who neglected to follow up had longer searches.

When job hunters were asked why they failed to follow up with this high level of decision maker, they said *"I don't want to bother them."* Job hunters could lose the opportunity by not continuing to make contact.

If weeks pass and you make no effort, the hiring manager will probably think:

1. **You found another job, or**
2. **You aren't really that interested.**

Either way, you're crossed off the list. All that work you did in networking to make contact wtih the hiring manager is wasted.

Reconnect with the hiring manager and converse like real people. If you can suggest something useful to the hiring manager, it also helps.

Samples:

- *I just wanted to touch base to let you know how interested I still am in your career opportunity. I know you said the wheels of hiring turn slowly these days, so I've been trying hard to control my enthusiasm. I look forward to hearing from you.*

- *I ran into Lillie Evans yesterday and she was telling me what a wonderful person you are to work for. I sincerely hope I have that opportunity.*

- *I came across an article on the Internet that I thought you might find useful for your company's needs. The link is _____. I am still very interested in being a part of your company.*

 Productivity Pointer

The Follow-Up Phone Call
- Follow-up calls should not be requests. Always have something useful to offer.
- Prepare an opening or a question that will provoke a response.
- Believe in what you are doing and put in the time and effort to prepare for these calls.
- Keep your voice friendly, cheerful and enthusiastic.

Rating Your Performance with Hiring Managers

Tracking your total number of conversations with hiring managers is an important part of search. Lee Hecht Harrison candidates average 20 to 30 conversations in the course of a search. However, the quality of those conversations is just as important as the quantity – and much more difficult to measure. The following is a simple device to rate the quality of your meetings.

Using a scale of 1 to 10 (with 10 the highest), rate yourself in the following areas:

1. How was my introduction? _____

2. Did I explore their needs and get new information? _____

3. Did I link my benefits to their needs? _____

4. Was I confident and professional? _____

5. How was my nonverbal communication? _____

6. Did I maintain good rapport with the hiring manager? _____

7. Were the hiring manager's comments positive? _____

8. Did I leverage a next meeting or conversation? _____

9. What is my overall satisfaction with the meeting? _____

HOW DID YOU DO?

If most of your rating numbers are in the 6 to 10 range, you are probably doing well. These meetings are not easy to conduct.

Look carefully at the lower ratings. Can you improve them? You may want to consider practicing with someone to get feedback on your approach and style.

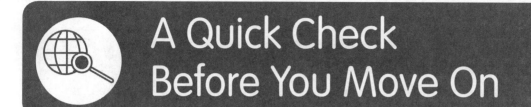

A Quick Check Before You Move On

Although it often takes only one person to make the decision to hire you, it usually takes many conversations with hiring managers to uncover the opportunity that leads to a job offer. As a result, you need to have (on average) 20 to 30 conversations with 20 to 30 different hiring managers before the offer you want is made.

Before you leave this milestone:

Go to Career Resource Network (CRN) to find:

- Tips on how to set up meetings with hiring managers

- Recommendations on how to conduct those meetings, using the SELL approach

- Samples of letters and email messages you can use to get the meeting and to follow up on it afterwards

- Suggestions on managing your Internet presence and how you may be able to connect with hiring managers through the use of social networking sites

Milestone 8

Consider Other Methods of Search

Why this Milestone is Important...

Talking to people to generate introductions to hiring managers remains the single most effective job search method, as substantiated by research data collected by Lee Hecht Harrison and other experts in the field. This simple method of people talking to people works for virtually anyone who makes the effort to use it in any of its many variations. Also called networking, this central search method is an integral part of completing the work of Milestones 5, 6 and 7.

Nonetheless, there are other so-called traditional methods of job search, which you should certainly consider. Perhaps some of them have worked for you or people you know in the past. It is simply a matter of including them in your work plan, trying them and then tracking and evaluating what does – and does not – work for you.

Evaluate and Consider All Search Methods

In all, there are seven search methods:

1. **Introductions, or simply talking to people you know**

2. **Advertisements and Internet job postings**

3. **Executive search firms, employment or staffing companies and temporary agencies**

4. **Job fairs and applications**

5. **Direct mail**

6. **Cold calling**

7. **Walk-in**

Of these seven, four are successful for only a small percentage of people in search: job fairs and applications, direct mail, cold calling and walk-in. These are discussed here. The remaining methods are useful to the majority of job hunters and are covered more extensively later in this chapter.

Cold Calling Works for a Few

Cold calling – calling people you do not know or have not been referred to by a contact – is a method that works for a small percentage of people. Success depends on a high level of skill, patience and persistence, because it typically takes many calls to get one personal meeting. Scripting the calls and then delivering them in an engaging way is also

important. Walking in unannounced to a potential employer is virtually out of the question for professionals and managers.

Direct Mail Works Better When Followed Up by Phone

Direct mail, or broadcast letters, involves sending letters or email correspondence to people who have never heard of you and who have no connection with you at all. It is a technique commonly used in product marketing. In essence, the hit rate to be considered successful (i.e., getting to a hiring manager) is low. It can be improved by combining direct mail with cold calling – following up on each letter or email with a telephone call. Using direct mail in job search can work for people who write effective letters and make persistent use of good telephone follow-up techniques. A sample of a direct mail letter is included later in this chapter.

Introductory Letters Work Better than Direct Mail

A distinction needs to be made between using the direct mail method and sending introductory letters or email messages to people with whom you have some kind of connection.

As described above, direct mail involves sending letters to organizations where you do not know anyone and have no introductions. Introductory letters are used when you have a referral from a contact or some other connection with the recipient. As such, it is simply part of talking to people. The reason for sending your letter is made clear at the beginning (Ian Smith suggested I contact you since you and I both attended State University at the same time). Introductory letters are generally much more successful than direct mail and well worth doing.

Questions to Explore

- *Who do I know who can recommend search firms or employment agencies that specialize in my industry or profession?*

- *Am I prepared to give my positioning statement and exit statement when contacting search firms and responding to openings by telephone?*

- *Which newspapers or trade journals should I check regularly for advertised positions?*

- *Is my resume available electronically for opportunities posted on the Internet? Do I have or need a scannable resume?*

- *Which Internet sites are appropriate for my type of profession? For my target industry?*

- *Are there job or career fairs available that would be worth my time to attend?*

Suggested Actions

- **Determine whether executive search firms or employment agencies are appropriate for you.** If they are, ask your networking contacts to recommend firms they have heard of or used. Then compile a list of appropriate firms and begin to contact them.

- **Decide which periodicals to check on a weekly basis.** Include your local newspaper(s) and national ones (such as *The New York Times* and the *Wall Street Journal*) if geographic location is not an issue, as well as any relevant industry or professional publication.

- **Research the job posting sites on the Internet and determine which ones are appropriate and relevant to you,** your profession and your targeted industry. Ask others in search about useful Internet sites.

- **Check the Internet sites of individual companies to determine which ones offer job openings,** especially the organizations on your target list.

- **Register and use LHH's resume posting site.** Also use the job bank on the CRN.

- **Check out local advertised job or career fairs** that may have potential for your search. Be wise with your time – do not travel too far or invest too much time unless the event is highly focused on the positions, industries and companies that you are interested in.

Working with Executive Search Firms

Executive search firms, also commonly referred to as recruiters or headhunters, work on the behalf of employers, not job seekers. They frequently recruit people who are employed, as well as active job seekers.

Search firms are local, national and even international in scope; some specialize by any combination of industry, function, geography or compensation level. Many handle only positions above $70,000; some handle positions only above $150,000. Fees for search firms – sometimes as much as 35% of base compensation – are always paid by the employer, never the job seeker.

Types of Executive Search Firms

Basically, executive search firms are classified by the way they earn their fees: retained or contingency. A retained search firm is hired by a company to identify, recruit and evaluate candidates for specific positions. A retained firm protects its reputation by being selective and carefully matching individuals to positions. Because they receive a retainer fee from the employer, they are paid whether their candidates are hired or not.

Contingency search firms receive a fee contingent on finding the person who is eventually hired for a job. A contingency firm might refer a number of people to a company to ensure that one of its candidates is selected for the position. They are paid only if a candidate is hired and may not be as selective in matching candidates to positions as a retained firm.

Search Firm Sourcing

When a search firm receives an assignment from an employer, one of the first steps it takes is to develop a list of people who can suggest possible job candidates. This is called sourcing and may involve some of the following sources:

- Major competitors
- Customers
- Suppliers
- Trade association executives
- Government or regulatory officials
- Faculty at major universities
- Consultants, contractors, service organizations
- Trade publication editors
- Lawyers, accountants, financiers (who specialize in an industry)

One of your tasks, therefore, in getting the word out is to make sure that the sources search firms use know about you and will propose your name if approached by a search firm.

Selecting Executive Search Firms

Identify reputable search firms by asking other job seekers, networking contacts or any human resources people you know if they can refer you to local search firms that specialize in your industry, profession and compensation level.

You can also research search firms using the Directory of Executive Recruiters and other directories and, of course, Internet sources. Other sources are the national and local Yellow Pages available online as well as in print.

In selecting which executive search firms to contact, consider the following:

- geographic area(s) they serve
- industries or sub-industries they specialize in
- kind(s) of jobs they fill

This information can be obtained by calling the individual firms or by checking print and online directories of executive search firms.

Guidelines for Using Search Firms

The following guidelines apply to employment agencies as well as to executive search firms:

1. **Present yourself as if you were on an actual job interview.** Remember: search firms work for and initially screen candidates for employers.

2. **Never pay a fee to a search firm or agency.** Beware of firms soliciting their services.

3. **Bring copies of your resume to any meeting you have with search firms.** Be prepared to explain your professional objective. If you have more than one objective, use only the one most appropriate to that particular firm. Also be prepared to discuss your preferred duties and responsibilities, targeted companies/industries and geographical preferences.

4. **Accept career advice cautiously.** Since these firms work for the employer, they may have a conflict of interest in giving you advice.

5. **State your salary expectations clearly at the outset.** They will not deal with you without this information. If you state a base salary, also mention benefits, performance awards and other compensation package requirements.

6. **Determine precisely what a search firm or employment agency plans to do to assist you** and how they intend to market you. Insist that they do not send your resume to any company without your prior consent. If they refuse this request, or if you do not receive the kind of service you anticipated, find another company.

7. **Make yourself known to probable search firm sources.**

 Tips and Techniques

Search Firms and Networking

One advantage of executive search firms is that they can quickly put you in a position of being one of a small number of final candidates for an open position appropriate to your skills and experience. A disadvantage is that you could find yourself in that situation without adequate preparation for interviewing, negotiating or making a decision on an offer.

Before, or soon after you send a mailing to a search firm, you need to do the research and especially the networking necessary to:

- Understand your targeted industries well enough to see where individual companies fit in.
- Get acquainted with a core group of organizations in each industry.
- Establish a sense of your current market value in each targeted industry so you can tell if an offer is high or low and have some ammunition for negotiations.

This preparation will establish an information context within which you will present yourself more effectively, negotiate knowledgeably and make the best decisions.

Using Contract and Temporary Agencies

CONTRACT AGENCIES

Typically, contract agencies hire quality people to provide professional services to businesses. A contract agency can benefit you by providing another source of job opportunities as contract work assignments or regular full-time job opportunities. Employers turn to contract agencies to provide the skills necessary to support and manage programs or services in a particular area or for a particular project. Many contract agencies also fill some full-time positions. Some examples of when a contract agency would be used would be: mergers, acquisitions or divestitures, sudden shifts in market or product focus or seasonable staffing pressures.

Some contract agencies also have a "registry" and website to advertise contract opportunities. The registry matches your work desires and preferences to opportunities presented by the contract agency. It usually requires that you fill out an online profile. Most contract assignments and regular full-time positions offer competitive pay packages and as a contractor, many agencies also offer some benefits.

Often contract agencies specialize in a particular profession. For example, a human resource contract agency might look for HR professionals that have expertise in staffing, compensation, consulting or assessment of HR management effectiveness who can implement and manage HR programs for projects. They might also look for an HR Director to fill a new position in an actively growing biotechnology company. Contract agencies usually ask applicants to sign a short contract (normally part of the application). You should not sign any contract that might obligate you to pay a fee.

Most good agencies clearly indicate that their listed positions are "fee paid" by the employer.

STAFFING OR TEMPORARY AGENCIES

Increasingly, staffing or temporary employment agencies are expanding far beyond administrative and hourly workers and are placing attorneys, financial professionals and even executives on a short-term basis.

Sometimes these project assignments lead to long-term employment; sometimes they do not. For many in transition, it is an option worth exploring since it is one way to get into a company and try it on for size. It is also a way to expand your contacts within a company.

Answering Internet Postings and Advertisements

Classified advertisements and Internet postings are placed by employers, employment agencies and search firms. Although many organizations place advertisements in major newspapers and websites in their attempts to recruit, studies suggest that only about one in 10 job seekers accept positions offered in ads or postings.

You should always respond when you see something that appeals to you. The reason is simple: responding to ads and postings represents a relatively small time investment on your part. Take the time to look through the classified and business sections of your local and national newspapers, particularly the Sunday editions. Many major newspapers are available online. Also check trade and professional journals; some of them are also available online. Studies show that of all the positions filled by companies from online sources, company websites were by far the largest source.

If you answer advertisements or postings and get no response, do not be concerned. Because of the expense involved, most employers respond only to those who pass the first screening. You should not expect an overall hit rate (i.e., invitations to interview as a percentage of applications) above the 3% to 10% range.

If you consistently have a hit rate above 10%, it is probably a sign your qualifications, paperwork and target market are extraordinary. On the other hand, if you are responding to numerous appropriate opportunities and have a hit rate below 3%, you should recheck your qualifications and consider revising your resume.

In the case of online postings, respond to those that are appropriate for you but do not focus a disproportionate amount of energy on them. It may appear there are more opportunities, but there is also more competition and your response rate may be low.

There are a large number of websites with job postings. Ask other job seekers and networking contacts for referrals to appropriate online sites. If you are using the Internet, the single most important thing you can do is to check the employment listings of the individual websites of your target companies.

Tips and Techniques

Answering an Internet Posting

When answering an Internet posting, be sure you use the right subject line. "Seeking employment" is not an acceptable subject. If you are responding to an advertisement, use the job title or job code cited in the job posting to make it easy for your email to be recognized and routed to the appropriate person. Remember: It only takes a second for someone to delete an email message. Think before you respond!

Guidelines for Answering Internet Postings and Advertisements

PREPARATION

- **Read each listing carefully,** weighing each word. Remember: your goal is to decipher the message so that you are assured of being on target in your response.

- **The response forms for Internet job postings vary.** Follow the instructions listed for individual postings. (See the chapter for Milestone 3 for guidelines for preparing resumes electronically.)

- **Assess each job requirement** and relate your experience, qualifications and accomplishments to the requirement.

- **When a contact name is not listed,** call the company and try to get the name of a specific person to whom the letter can be written.

- **Always send a cover letter with your resume.** If you are responding by email, include your cover letter as part (page one) of your resume file, and check individual requirements for submitting information electronically.

- **If an ad is very attractive and your resume is not an obvious match for it,** you may choose to send a two-page letter with no resume or even write a new resume for it. If you use a letter, it must be as easy to scan as a resume and include pertinent facts, such as dates, employers and job titles. This time consuming approach is worthwhile only on those rare occasions when the "perfect job" shows up in a blind ad.

ADMINISTRATION AND FOLLOW-UP

- **Keep a copy of your letter and the advertisement** (or print out the online listing). Create a file for your responses so you have a record for follow-up purposes.

- **If the ad is open,** enter the company on your target list and pursue it by other means as well.

- **Track your hit rate for ads.**

CONTENT

- **Begin your letter by identifying the newspaper, magazine, website or journal,** the date of the advertisement and the position title. If you are responding by email, consider using an eye-catching subject line that includes the job or reference number.

- **Develop the body of your letter by describing your qualifications,** experience and accomplishments as they relate to the job requirements covered in the ad.

- **Do not mention any part of the job for which you do not qualify.**

- **Include additional information,** such as relevant community or professional activities, only if it makes you appear more attractive for the position.

- **Conclude your letter positively by stating that you look forward to a meeting.** With an open ad, take the responsibility for following up by giving a time when you will call to arrange an appointment for a meeting.

STYLE

- **Be concise and to the point.** Keep it to one page. Eight out of 10 human resources professionals say they spend less than an average of one minute reading a cover letter.

- **Write in a straightforward manner** that reflects your natural style of communication.

- **Always carefully check your letter** for the correct name and address, misspellings, grammatical mistakes or typos. Errors found in a cover letter could remove you from the pool of possible candidates.

Should You Provide a Salary History?

When answering advertisements and Internet postings, try not to provide salary information. Providing your last salary or a salary history may limit your ability to negotiate a salary later.

It will almost certainly eliminate you if your salary is significantly different from what an employer has in mind. Too high a number could make you overqualified, too low a number could make you seem underqualified. You risk being screened out on the number alone, without consideration of your real qualifications.

On online applications, leave the salary question space blank, if possible. You want to defer this discussion as long as possible. The more opportunities you have to reveal your true worth before placing a dollar figure on your talents, the better.

However, in order to complete some online applications, you must put an exact figure or you cannot proceed with the application. A salary history does not mean going back to your first job at your first company. It can be the history in your last company. For example: "I started at $_____ with ABC Company and was earning $_____ at the time of downsizing."

Some applications also might ask what range you are looking for. If possible, also leave this blank. If you must provide an answer in order to proceed, be prepared to live with the answer you supply. Don't expect to negotiate later for a figure above the highest point on your range. You've set your mark, and you can bet your potential employer will not forget it.

Key Points to Remember:

- If you are seen as a strong candidate, most employers will not screen you out because you omitted your salary history.

- Salary is just one piece of your compensation package. There are many other negotiating factors such as title, vacation, relocation expenses, stock options and more.

- The request for salary history can sometimes be finessed by responding with a salary range. Just be sure you like the bottom numbers in that range because you are indicating a willingness to accept it.

- If your research makes you confident that your current or most recent compensation is close to what the prospective employer pays, and if you are not planning to try for a significant increase, provide the numbers requested.

More on Handling the Salary Question

When you've made it to the next step in the process and have your actual interview with your potential employer, you'll have to address the salary question again.

Look in Milestone 9 (Interview, Cultivate Offers and Negotiate) for the best ways of dealing with that situation.

 Tips and Techniques

Ads and Online Postings as Sources

Advertisements and online postings can be used as a source of information. They can tell you...

- which companies and industries are hiring.

- what titles are currently in use.

- what words to use in describing your qualifications.

- typical job requirements and descriptions, and sometimes salary information.

Cover Letters for Ads and Online Postings

Always include a cover letter, if possible, when responding to ads and online postings. Even online job postings usually provide a space for you to insert your letter. This enables you to connect with your potential employer on a personal level, rather than just through your resume.

Cover Letter Format

Date

Address

Salutation

Paragraph one: Mention the title of the job, where you heard of the opening (date and name of publication or website), and that your resume is included. Make a statement that you believe you are a strong candidate and/or include relevant facts from your research to demonstrate your specific interest and knowledge about the company.

Paragraph two: Briefly describe your professional background, focusing on specific skills, activities, accomplishments and experiences. Select several significant requirements from the ad and match your accomplishments, qualifications and experience to them, making sure the match between their stated needs and your qualifications is obvious. Consider using bullets to make them stand out.

Paragraph three: Optional additional information on your qualifications.

Paragraph four: Reinforce your qualifications and suggest next actions. Include your phone number or email address. Thank the reader for his/her time and consideration.

Closing

Name

Enclosure

 # Response to an Ad

---

Vice President, Sales
Immediate opening for proven sales executive to lead national sales team. Successful candidate will manage national sales in addition to training, motivating and developing a sales staff of 30. Must be goal-oriented, enjoy challenge and have proven background in leading sales teams and meeting/exceeding goals. Send cover letter and resume to Ms. Loretta Levine, ABC Corporation, 101 Parker Corporate Park, Stamford. CT 06901.

Name
Address
City / State / Zip
Telephone Number • Email Address

Date

Ms. Loretta Levine
ABC Corporation
101 Parker Corporate Park
Stamford, CT 06901

Dear Ms. Levine:

In response to your February 20 advertisement in *The New York Times* for a Vice President, Sales, I am enclosing my resume. As a goal-oriented sales executive, I think you will find that my background and experience closely match those mentioned in your advertisement.

For the past five years, as Eastern Region Sales Manager for the Business Division of McArthur Publishing, I managed a sales department with responsibilities for hiring, training and motivating a team of 23 sales professionals. Within one year, everyone on the sales staff had met or exceeded their quotas and we exceeded our sales targets by 15%.

While with Gray Communications as Sales Manager of their Educational Products Division, I was responsible for managing and motivating a sales staff that doubled their renewal sales in the first six months. In addition, I developed and implemented a new compensation and incentive plan, which was successfully duplicated in two other sales functions within the company.

As you will see from my resume, there are other areas that address your requirements. I would appreciate the opportunity to discuss them with you and will call you next Thursday to see when we might meet and discuss how I can contribute to ABC's continued leadership in its field. Please feel free to call me at 203-555-1111.

Sincerely,

Name

Enclosure

SAMPLE Response to an Online Ad

XYZ Systems

Code/Title: HR-DHR 08491 - Director, Human Resources

Location: Palo Alto, California

Description: Head up our efforts to establish a top-notch HR Department. In this key role you will function as a business partner in organizational development, compensation, benefits, training, employee relations, recruiting and human resources administrative functions. Specifically, you will establish operations strategies, policies and programs that meet departmental objectives, ensure compliance with applicable regulatory requirements and direct human resources team to provide customer-oriented support to management and employees.

Requirements: BA/BS or equivalent; MA preferred. Minimum of eight years of directly related experience, with successful record managing multi-human resources functions in an international company. Minimum of two years of recent management experience working for high tech manufacturing company. Strong generalist background, with emphasis on organizational change and management development. Minimum bilingual skills in Spanish. Experience dealing with employees at all levels and with visa and work permits for foreign nationals necessary. Relocation assistance is not available.

To apply for this position, please fill in this form and click on the SUBMIT button below.

Name	
Address	
City	
State/Province	
Zip	
Phone	
Email	
Position title	Director, Human Resources
Job Code	HR-DHR 08491

Your resume can be uploaded in any of the following formats: DOC, DOCX, RTF, PDF, TXT, HTML. Or you can paste a plain text version in the text area below. You can also use the text area for a cover letter.

(Submit)   (Clear Fields)

Direct Mail Letter

Name
Address
City / State / Zip
Telephone Number • Email Address

Date

Mr. Frederick D. Hubbard
Nationwide Dairy Company
111 Main Street
Burlington, VT 05670

Dear Mr. Hubbard:

I have been following Nationwide Dairy's advertising and promotions, and am impressed with the innovative marketing strategies you have employed to build a loyal consumer following and gain supermarket shelf space.

You have succeeded in differentiating Nationwide Dairy by recognizing that consumers are intelligent, know what they want and have a sense of humor. This year's well-executed "Say Cheese" photo contest helped solidify a uniquely positive brand image, even in the face of significantly higher promotional spending by your competitors. At this stage, I imagine that a key strategic issue for you might lie in finding ways to continue to build your brand image.

In my 15 years in packaged goods marketing management, I have successfully dealt with the unique challenges facing similar products in fiercely competitive markets. For Southside Food's D-D-Licious Bubble Gum, I developed a strategy for introducing new flavors that resulted in a 22% market share gain and $25 million in incremental business. Later, as Group Product Manager for NuWay's Pet Foods Division, I oversaw the creation and launch of Curious Cat, which became a $70 million brand in just two years.

I would value the opportunity to meet with you to discuss your plans for business development, the organization of your marketing function, and ways in which I might contribute my own strategic marketing skills to the furthering of your exciting business.

I will call you early next week to set up a time to meet at your convenience. I look forward to an enlightening discussion.

Sincerely,

Name

Attending Job or Career Fairs

Keep in mind that career fairs should be just one small part of your entire job search process; however, they can be a successful method to check out target companies, learn of job openings and network. There are many types of job and career fairs, but they all have one common focus: It's a chance for a company to meet and screen a large volume of potential job candidates.

When you become aware of a job or career fair you need to first decide if it is worth the time to attend, if it's in your profession or industry, and whether the time spent is worth the results you might obtain. Regardless of how you plan to take advantage of your next job expo, there are strategies to help you use this technique wisely.

Strategies for Job or Career Fairs

Preparation

- **Find out in advance what companies will be there.** Determine if there are companies that are currently on your target list or in the same general industry. There is usually a website that you can visit to see a list of companies that will be attending a specific fair.

- **Research the companies you are most interested in and decide which ones you will approach.** Don't waste time with companies that do not interest you.

- **Be prepared for some kind of real interview** because what you will encounter at job fairs are multiple, mini-interviews.

What to Bring

- **Lots of copies of your resume** – at least two copies for each employer you plan to select.

- **A briefcase so that you can store the materials you gather as you go.** A briefcase adds to your professional appearance.

- **Lots of business cards**.

Working the Maze

Most job fairs are a maze of corridors, displays, tables, signs and people. Here are some pointers:

- **Work your priority companies first.** It's better to wait in a line and get your top five choices out of the way early than to hit a bunch of low priorities and meet your targets late in the day.

- **Before you get into a line for a targeted employer,** pick up the materials displayed on the tables and read them for possible questions to ask.

Strategies for Job or Career Fairs

Types of Interviews

You may only have two to five minutes to market yourself and protect yourself from being screened out. Be prepared with a brief "Tell Me About Yourself" statement that highlights the key benefits that you can offer the organization. Typically, there are three types of interviews conducted at career or job fairs:

- **Screening Interview.** This is your first encounter with the recruiter. It will be brief so you need to make the most of the time allotted. Be prepared to answer typical questions such as: *What are you looking for at the fair?* Or: *Can you tell me a little about yourself and what you are looking for?* Get the recruiter's business card.

- **Mini-Interview.** Some companies conduct mini-interviews that might last 5-10 minutes. Be prepared to use your positioning statement and elaborate on parts of your resume. All the guidelines and rules for interviewing apply except you need to position yourself as an excellent candidate in less time than at a regular full interview. Get the recruiter's business card.

- **Full Interview.** Although rare, some companies do full-blown interviews on-site. These might last 20-30 minutes. Your goal is to pass this interview with flying colors and be asked to come to the company locations for more interviewing. Again, get the recruiter's business card.

Questions to Ask at Job or Career Fairs

Remember, a career fair is a two-way process and you should be evaluating these companies as much as they are evaluating you. As with any situation where you find yourself with a potential employer, you must be prepared to ask insightful questions of recruiters at job and career fairs. Which questions should you ask? It depends on the recruiter, on your interest and knowledge of the company, and how much time you have with the recruiter. You will want to ask questions that are designed to give you the chance to respond to the recruiter's answer with information on how you perfectly fit what the company is looking for in an employee. Some examples:

- *What kinds of skills and experience do you look for in the employees you hire?*

- *What are the characteristics of your most successful employees?*

A great concluding question for you to ask is,

- *"What do I need to do to obtain a second interview with your company?"*

What to Do Next

Follow-up is critical and often neglected. Within 24 hours, write a note (handwritten, word processed or email) to every recruiter you met with. In the letter, thank the recruiter for their time, restate your interest and qualifications for the position, reiterate your interest in a second interview and make a promise to follow up the letter with a phone call (and then make sure you call!). You probably should enclose another copy of your resume to be sure. After the job or career fair, also reassess your target list and add or delete companies as needed.

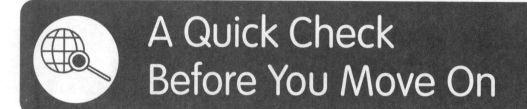

A Quick Check
Before You Move On

Getting the word out by talking to people remains the most effective job search method, but it's worth some of your time to check out other methods of search, including contacting recruiters, posting your resume, or finding job leads on the Internet or in other media.

Before you leave this milestone:

Go to Career Resource Network (CRN) to find:

• Discussions and tips on how to identify and contact recruiters, find job leads, respond to published ads or job board listings, use direct mail and post your resume

• Samples of letters and email messages you can use in these efforts

• Access to Lee Hecht Harrison's powerful resume-posting tools to help you reach employers and recruiters

• Tips on building your brand through effectively managing your Internet presence and maintaining a personal website to reference in discussions or correspondence

As a general rule, you should "duck" the salary question in job board listings and in responding to ads, as that discussion should be part of the negotiation process. However, you will want to reveal your last salary and your salary expectations to recruiters, as that's an important element in their consideration of you vis-à-vis the positions they're trying to fill.

Manage transition

Get results

Manage Transition

Manage Transition includes Milestones 9 and 10. It is the phase of the AIM process where you are getting results.

In most searches, about 20% of the 20 to 30 conversations with hiring managers become formal interviews or very serious conversations about jobs. Once you have negotiated and accepted the right offer, you begin managing your career in a new organization.

Milestone	Outcome	Pages
9. **Interview, Cultivate Offers and Negotiate**	**You have located, negotiated and accepted the position you want.** The work of Milestones 5, 6, 7, 8 and 9 involve the implementation of your marketing plan.	139-170
10. **Transition into a New Position**	**You have closed out your search in ways that position you to manage your career effectively in the future.** You receive specific and significant positive feedback in the first 90 days in your new position, and your first performance review is better than average.	171-179

Milestone 9

Interview, Cultivate Offers and Negotiate

Why this Milestone is Important...

If you are like most people, you will go through the interviewing, cultivating offers and negotiating phase several times before successfully completing this milestone. On the way to accepting a great new position, the average Lee Hecht Harrison client talks to 20 to 30 hiring managers. About 20% of these discussions, or four to six for the average client, are actual interviews. Since only one of them produces an offer that is accepted, we can also say that the average client succeeds on the fifth interview.

Effective Preparation Increases Your Odds of Success

Whether you succeed in your fifth interview – or your second or tenth – depends on a combination of your preparation, skills and timing. Your considerable work completing the previous eight milestones has prepared you to succeed in this important phase. The skills and strategy you need to be successful in this phase are covered in this chapter.

An interview is a serious discussion between you and a hiring manager about a particular position. The most common misunderstanding of job interviews is that the role of the person being interviewed is to be passive and to simply react to the interviewer. In fact, successful candidates are usually just as active and often better prepared than their interviewers.

You Need to Know How to Predict and Prepare for Interview Topics

As a candidate, your job is to get your core message across to the hiring manager, regardless of that person's skills as an interviewer. This is not difficult to do because much of what happens in interviews is predictable. You can predict with a great deal of accuracy many of the questions you will be asked. You can and should prepare the general message you want to transmit. You can and should prepare questions on the information you want to collect.

Prepare to Answer Behavior-Based Interview Questions

Employment professionals these days are commonly trained in what is called behavior-based interviewing. In behavior-based interviewing, the interviewer asks questions designed to elicit accounts of your behavior that illustrate the nature and extent of your competencies and your particular approach in applying those competencies to real world work situations.

Your most important preparation for a behavior-based interview is planning your core message using your competency list and SOAR (Situation, Obstacles, Action and Results) stories. You prepared your competency list and SOAR stories as part of your preparation in the chapters for Milestones 2 and 4.

A well-prepared candidate might go into an interview with six SOAR stories prepared for each of six competencies, for a total of 36 different stories. Naturally, you will probably not use all 36 of these stories in any single interview. However, a wide range of prepared stories allows you to select those most appropriate to the interviewer's expressed needs and most relevant to questions asked.

You Have One Hour to Get Your Core Message Across Convincingly

Advance preparation of your SOAR stories enables you to relate them accurately and concisely so that you offer more concrete evidence of your competencies in one hour than the unprepared candidate.

Even when being interviewed by an interviewer who does not use behavior-based techniques, your best strategy remains the same: Use your accomplishment stories to answer questions whenever possible. It is a powerful technique because it provides demonstrable evidence to convince the interviewer – and aid the interviewer in convincing others – that you are the best choice.

Why this Milestone is Important...

This milestone chapter organizes predictable questions into categories and suggests strategies for dealing with each of the categories. Once you have your SOAR stories prepared, working with these categories of predictable questions can make you very effective – even in your first interview.

Offers Come Faster if You Know How to Cultivate Them

During the interview, as well as before and after it, you need to be working on cultivating offers. Cultivating the offer actually begins with the first conversations with people inside of your target companies. The ultimate aim of any conversation with a hiring manager at any stage of the search is to cultivate an offer. Early on, this is best done by clearly displaying your interest in the organization and your relevant skills, as well as by building relationships and collecting information to build a case for your candidacy.

During and after the interview, the single best way to cultivate offers, in addition to effectively displaying your competencies, is simply saying: I really want this job. A common mistake made in post-interview follow-ups is asking only about your status as a candidate. It is not enough to simply ask if a decision has been made yet. You need to cultivate the offer by confirming your qualifications for the position, providing additional information if necessary and, of course, continuing to express interest in the position.

You Need to Know What to Negotiate

When an offer is received, the first thing to remember is that everything about it is potentially negotiable. The higher the position and the smaller the organization, the more likely it is that more elements of the offer can be successfully negotiated.

At the same time, the organization is also free to negotiate and make adjustments in response to your negotiating strategy. Naturally, this includes the possibility of withdrawing their offer, just as you can walk away from their offer. So you must be clear about what you feel is important enough to negotiate and what you will accept.

You Need to Know How to Negotiate

In negotiating a new position, it is essential that you take a win-win stance. After all, you are negotiating with an organization with which you hope to have a long-term relationship and with an individual who will be your next boss. An important part of your strength in the negotiating process is the amount of information you have on the industry, the organization and the people to whom you are talking. Therefore, the more work you have done in advance in terms of being clear about what you will and will not accept, the better your position.

Questions to Explore

- *Have I clarified what I need to know about the organization, the position and my next boss?*

- *Am I effectively implementing my communications strategy regardless of the skill (or lack of skill) of the interviewers? Am I communicating all of my assets in interviews?*

- *Am I pursuing a variety of ways of uncovering the information I need, including tapping my network and accessing available databases?*

- *Do I have a negotiating strategy? Have I determined what I want most in my next position in terms of my role, responsibilities, compensation and environment? Have I prioritized my wants and needs so that I am prepared to negotiate?*

- *Do I have reliable data regarding compensation for someone in my position so I know how to position myself when negotiating?*

Suggested Actions

- **Anticipate questions you might be asked.** Practice your answers, perhaps even videotape them so you can review your performance. Make sure to include a discussion about compensation in your practice.

- **Develop a list of questions you want to ask and practice them.**

- **Be prepared to demonstrate how you have made a difference in the past at other organizations.** Review your accomplishment stories and prepare more that are relevant to the organization and the position, if necessary. Practice these stories so they become more conversational.

- **After every discussion with a hiring manager, note what you have learned about their needs and expectations.** Follow up with email, phone call or letter to emphasize how you can address their needs and make a difference.

- **After every discussion, take notes about your performance to determine what went well** and how you might be better prepared to make your case.

- **Make a list of your needs and wants and prioritize them** so you know what you will insist on and what you are willing to sacrifice.

- **Research the market to determine normal compensation levels for positions like the ones you are seeking.**

The Strategic Interviewing Process

The interview is the single most important step in getting a job – it is the culmination of all of your good planning and thorough preparation. It is also a process over which you can have a fair amount of control as long as you have a strategy. That strategy needs to include being prepared, knowing what to expect, eliciting needs, presenting competencies and handling questions. The interview is your opportunity to market and sell yourself by demonstrating what your skills, experience and qualifications can do for the company.

The Four C's: What the Interviewer and You Are Looking For

Part of your strategy is to understand the interviewer's strategy. A traditional interviewer is looking for three basic things – competence, compatibility and chemistry. You are looking for the same things, plus compensation. This is your final check to see if this really is the right job for you.

Competence

Interviewer | **You**

Can you do the job? Do you have the ability to perform the specific functions of the position effectively? The interviewer is looking for evidence that your experience, skills and competencies match the position and the organization.

Can I do the job? Do I have the ability to perform the specific functions of the position effectively? You may want a job that stretches you a bit, but you do not want one you cannot handle. Even more important, are the competencies required the ones you want to exercise every day? Is this what you want to do?

Compatibility

Interviewer | **You**

Can you do the job here? Will you relate effectively to the diverse employees in the organization? Usually, you will have several interviews with the hiring manager as well as others in the organization in order to determine your compatibility with the organizational culture.

Can I do the job there? Will I relate effectively to the diverse employees in the organization? How do I feel about the organizational culture? Is it consistent with my values? Do I want to work in a place like that?

Chemistry

Interviewer | **You**

Can you do the job with us? Do we like you enough? Do you like us enough? Interpersonal chemistry is very important in the selection process. Even if you are the most qualified person on earth, there needs to be the feeling that they like you enough to spend a minimum of 40 hours a week with you – and vice versa.

Can I do the job with them? Do I like these people? Do I like them enough? Interpersonal chemistry is very important in a job, especially with your immediate supervisor and peers. All in all, are these people you will be happy working with?

Compensation

You

Can I do the job for what they will pay? This is always the last question in the process, since raising it too soon can create problems for you. But the compensation – in dollars, benefits and satisfaction – should certainly be a key item on your list.

Types of Interviews

A big part of preparing yourself for the interviewing process is being aware of the types of interviews to expect. In addition to the face-to-face interview with a hiring manager, there are other types of interviews:

1. The screening interview

Frequently a company will conduct a screening – or initial – interview to determine whether or not you should be considered more seriously as a candidate before engaging in a longer, more in-depth meeting. A screening interview can take place in person or by telephone. A human resources professional or a hiring manager (or even an external recruiter) might conduct it. Whatever, it is still an interview and your goal needs to be to keep yourself in the running and be asked back for another interview. It is rare that an offer is made at a first interview so it is in your interest to avoid or defer discussion of salary or benefits until you know more about the job and/or an offer is made.

2. The behavior-based interview

Behavior-based interviewing is a style of interviewing where the interviewer rates the evidence of job-related skills in two major areas, job (or technical) and performance skills, in order to match a person's skills to the job requirements. You need to respond to questions in ways that adapt your skills to the needs of the organization, keeping in mind that skill requirements differ from one organization to another.

3. The case interview

The case interview is often used by management-consulting firms and investment banking companies and is increasingly being used by other types of corporations as well. In a case interview, you are introduced to a business dilemma facing a particular company (often drawn from the interviewer's professional experience). You are asked to analyze the situation, identify key business issues and discuss how you would address the problems. The interviewer begins by giving you some basic facts and then asks you an open-ended or specific question. The interview proceeds as an open dialogue between you and the interviewer, with the interviewer guiding the discussion as you ask probing questions to uncover key information.

Case interviews are designed to scrutinize the skills that are especially important in management consulting and related fields: quantitative skills, analytical skills, problem-solving ability, communications skills, creativity, flexibility, the ability to think quickly under pressure, listening skills, business acumen, keen insight, interpersonal skills, the ability to synthesize findings, professional demeanor and powers of persuasion.

4. The group (or panel) interview

Group or panel interviews are meetings with more than one person at the same time in the same room (although there are occasions when they might be conducted by telephone). Group interviews are conducted for a variety of reasons: to allow all people involved in the hiring to interview you at the same time; to get a cross section of opinions; to see how you fit into a particular group; and to see how you handle talking with several people at the same time.

A group interview requires that you adopt more of a presentation style to your answers and questions. Try to remember each person's name and title (or ask for business cards before or after the meeting) and direct answers or questions to individuals as appropriate. Maintain good eye contact with each person when answering questions. Shake hands with all members of the group when entering and leaving the interview, and send a follow-up letter to your primary contact, acknowledging the others in attendance.

Types of Interviews

5. The telephone interview

Telephone interviews are becoming a more common practice and can occur in a number of ways. As just mentioned, they can be part of the screening process as a way of speeding up the initial selection, part of a conversation with a contact or hiring manager that moves into a discussion of an opening or a planned event when both parties agree in advance to speak at a future time. In all cases, you need to be prepared and conduct yourself as you would in a face-to-face meeting except you have the advantage of using and taking notes.

From the employer's standpoint, the telephone interview is effective for eliminating unqualified candidates with a minimum commitment of time and resources. For you, a telephone interview has its advantages and disadvantages. One big advantage is that you can work from notes and other written materials.

Screening interviews on the telephone can happen when you least expect them. If you receive a call that you perceive to be a screening interview and you are not totally prepared or it is not convenient for you, explain that this is not the most opportune time and ask to reschedule the call.

A telephone interview is just as important as a face-to-face one, and you want to be sure you are prepared and not distracted. An experienced interviewer typically begins the interview with an overview of the job, a reference to your resume and perhaps an explanation of why you have been selected as a candidate for the position (e.g., identifying some areas of your experience that qualify you for the job). A telephone interview usually lasts between 10 and 30 minutes, with questions being asked about your education, job skills, technical knowledge and work experience.

6. The video interview

More and more companies are turning to video interviews, via the Web, to further screen potential hires before flying them to meet the boss. In some cases, this also could serve as the final interview before the hiring decision is made.

With budget cuts these days, it only makes business sense to save on the expenses of airlines, lodging and food. That is not to mention the valuable time required of managers for the actual interview process.

A hiring manager may like what you said on the phone but isn't totally convinced. The next phase of the screening process could be the recorded video interview or a live virtual interview.

The recorded interview may be done at a video conferencing center, a recruiter's office or even your home. Don't worry if you don't have a webcam – it will be sent to you, complete with

instructions. You may even be allowed to keep it. Typically, you respond to 15-20 questions entered into the system from your potential employer within an allotted time frame – usually two minutes between each question.

Also through a webcam, a live video conference can be held between the candidate and the hiring manager or a panel of managers. Be as prepared as if you were walking into your future employer's office. Dress professionally and be prepared with your answers.

While this may seem intimidating, think of it as your chance to shine. A resume, no matter how well written, may not do you justice. A phone interview also may stop short of revealing the person you really are. This could provide a great way to market yourself, so take advantage of the opportunity.

Guidelines for Interviewing

1. PREPARING FOR THE INTERVIEW

- **Conduct additional research on the company** so that you are thoroughly aware of its reputation, size, products, history, philosophy and culture. Get the names and titles of the decision-makers you should meet. If at all possible, try to get inside information about the position and the people with whom you would be working. Visit the company's website.

- **Based on your research, tailor your accomplishment stories** to the position and organization, and prepare your own questions about the company to ask during the interview.

- **Determine exactly who will be conducting the interview**, including title, division and line of authority, either before the interview or during the first few moments of the meeting.

- **Take your research notes on the company,** previous correspondence, your list of questions and several copies of your resume to the meeting. Take a copy of your reference list as well, in case you are asked for them.

2. CONDUCTING THE INTERVIEW

- **Arrive a little early to get a sense of the company culture** (décor, how people dress) and to review any company materials that might be in the reception area.

- **Establish how much time is planned for the interview,** and determine how much time you will have to ask questions.

- **Uncover as much information as possible about the position** before going into detail about your background.

- **Listen carefully to the questions** and make sure you understand what is being asked. If the question is not clear, ask for clarification.

- **Always respond to questions with positive answers** and by matching specific accomplishments and qualifications to the job. Keep your answers to no-win questions brief.

- **Tailor and expand on the positioning statement** you did in Milestone 3 to the needs of the job. It is the best way to respond to the request: Tell me about yourself.

- **Postpone salary discussions until an offer is made,** if at all possible. If you are pressed to give your salary, try to avoid naming a figure. You might lose your leverage for future negotiations.

- **If you are asked to meet other people in the organization,** determine their relationship to the position as well as their names, titles, division and lines of authority. Do not be afraid to ask a few polite questions when introduced to uncover the information. Ask for a business card.

- **Do not dominate the interview** – or let the interviewer dominate it. Keep it interactive.

- **Before concluding an interview,** make sure all of your questions are answered and ask what the next steps will be.

Guidelines for Interviewing

3. CONCLUDING THE INTERVIEW

- **Summarize the meeting with a variation of your positioning statement,** highlighting your interest in and value to the position and the organization.

- **You may wish to use a trial close,** such as: What are your thoughts about my candidacy for this position? This will help you determine if there are any key qualifications you forgot to sell or if the interviewer has doubts you need to address.

- **Arrange a specific date and time for your next contact with them,** rather than leaving it entirely in their hands. If you do this, you will be in a strong position to follow up. Knowing the timing will also help you manage the rest of your search.

- **If it is not clear what the next step will be, ask the interviewer:** What will the next step in your hiring process be? Or: When may I expect to hear from you again? These questions indicate an interest and desire on your part to continue the process.

- **Immediately after the interview,** make notes about information you gathered, especially the organization's needs and expectations. And take notes about your own performance to determine what went well and how you might be better prepared to answer questions in the future.

- **Send follow-up letters** within 24 hours of the interview.

4. IMPORTANCE OF NON-VERBAL COMMUNICATION

- **Offer a firm handshake,** smile sincerely, make eye contact and let the interviewer know you are glad to be there.

- **Establish rapport as quickly as possible** with friendly and enthusiastic small talk. Pay a compliment if you can or comment favorably on something in the office (the view, family photos, personal mementos) if you are sure the office or item belongs to the interviewer.

- **Select clothing appropriate to the corporate culture of the organization,** erring on the side of conservative, and make sure it is in the best possible condition.

- **Pay special attention to your personal grooming:** your hair, makeup, shoes. If you wear jewelry, remember less is best.

- **Show interest, optimism and enthusiasm.** Maintain eye contact throughout the interview.

- **Listen carefully from the moment you arrive and throughout the interview.**

Note: Interviewers often make immediate judgments about applicants – sometimes within the first 30 to 60 seconds of a meeting. It stands to reason that your first impression should be that of a skilled professional.

Asking the Right Questions

Many books on interviewing will tell you that toward the end of a traditional interview, you will be given an opportunity to ask questions. However, a better way is to look for opportunities to ask questions throughout the interview, not just when asked what questions you have.

The interviewing process involves two-way communication. It is just as important for you to ask – as well as respond to – questions. Asking the right questions serves two purposes. First, it is the way to get the information you need to match your qualifications to the requirements of the job when answering questions. Second, it is the way to get the information you need to evaluate the position and make a decision as to whether it is the right one for you.

There are five significant areas you need to ask questions about in order to get information and evaluate the position. The subject areas are listed on the following page, along with the kinds of questions you can ask. Asking these questions throughout the interview increases the probability of a more interactive dialogue. An important caveat: Not all of these questions are appropriate to ask of all companies. You need to match the questions to the organization based on what you know about it and its culture.

Tips and Techniques

Traps to Avoid at the Interview

- Be careful not to show signs of nervousness, such as laughing, fidgeting or squirming. People are usually nervous during interviews, but you can control the amount of nervousness you display.

- Be confident rather than overly concerned with the possibility of rejection. Focus on what you can do for the employer. Remember, this is a two-way street – you need to see if you like them.

- Never be critical of a past employer or the performance of any employee there. Above all, avoid the temptation to speak negatively about a former supervisor.

- Rather than arguing, speak confidently, keeping the discussion friendly and open.

- Do not show irritation with delays or interruptions, even if you are irritated.

- Avoid apologizing or being defensive over things you cannot change and for which you are not responsible, such as your age, education or work history. Such areas are predictable and your approach should be planned and rehearsed.

- Admit if there is something you do not know. No one is totally knowledgeable.

- Avoid expressions such as "like" and "you know" and too many "er's" and "uh's." Take your time and think before you speak.

- Never underestimate the influence of a human resources employee or some other non-decision maker. View this individual as someone who may have influence (however small) with the hiring manager.

What to Ask in an Interview

1. **RESPONSIBILITIES OF THE POSITION**
   - *What are the major responsibilities of this position?*
   - *Does a job description exist for this position and, if so, may I see it?*
   - *Beyond the job description, what are your expectations?*
   - *How long has this position existed in the organization?*
   - *What would be the next career progression?*
   - *What situations need immediate attention?*
   - *What qualifications do you expect the successful candidate to have?*

2. **RESOURCES AVAILABLE TO ACCOMPLISH RESPONSIBILITIES**
   - *Can I meet the people who work in the department?*
   - *What experience, training and tenure do the employees in the department have?*
   - *Does the company provide training programs?*
   - *Does this department have its own budget?*
   - *What interdepartmental or corporate support is available to accomplish the department's goals?*

3. **LEVEL OF AUTHORITY**
   - *Whom would I be supervising in this position?*
   - *What are the reporting relationships?*
   - *How long has the supervisor of this position been with the company?*
   - *What is the supervisor's experience and training?*
   - *What are the established guidelines and procedures for making decisions in this position?*
   - *What would be the extent of my authority to carry out the responsibilities of this position?*
   - *Would I have the authority to hire/terminate employees in order to accomplish the goals?*
   - *Would I have direct input for the department budget? Would I be totally responsible for developing the budget while in this position?*

4. **PERFORMANCE MEASUREMENTS**
   - *What are the short- and long-term goals of the position, and how are they established?*
   - *Do you have an appraisal system? How does it work?*
   - *What is the most important contribution you would expect from me during the first six months?*
   - *How would successful performance be rewarded?*
   - *How often is performance reviewed in this position?*

5. **CORPORATE CULTURE**
   - *How would you describe the culture of the organization?*
   - *How would you describe the organization's management style?*
   - *Is the company environment formal or informal, structured or flexible?*
   - *Can you describe the interdepartmental relationships?*
   - *What has the turnover rate of the department been?*
   - *Why is this position open?*
   - *Are there any internal candidates being considered for this position?*
   - *Does your company support "green" initiatives?*

Interviewing Models

Traditional Interviewing
Conducted by the Interviewer

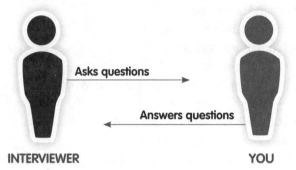

In the traditional interviewing model, the interviewer poses a question and you do your best to answer it.

This model places an inordinate amount of responsibility for the success of the meeting in the hands of the interviewer, leaving you to believe that the only goal of the interview is to correctly answer all of the interviewer's questions.

Strategic Interviewing
Conducted by You and the Interviewer

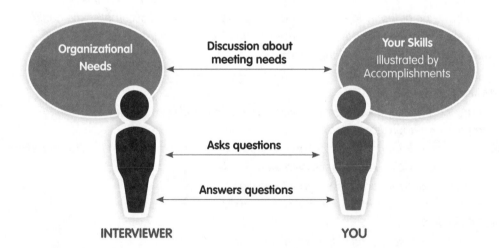

In this model, the question and answer process is still in the foreground. However, there is more of a dialogue about organizational needs and the needs of the hiring manager. This enables you to tailor your statements to address those needs, using appropriate accomplishment stories.

Tell Me About Yourself

Tell me about yourself is frequently used as an interview opener.

Use the positioning statement you constructed in the chapter for Milestone 3, focusing particularly on what you know the employer needs and selecting the most relevant material you have. The best way to respond to this type of request is to expand upon and tailor your positioning statement to match the needs of an organization.

Use the outline below as a guide:

I am a **(profession/level)** _____

_____

_____

with expertise in **(functions or capabilities)** _____

_____

_____

My strengths include **(unique professional qualities)** _____

_____

_____

Particular accomplishments or distinctions relevant to the position are _____

_____

_____

_____

I have worked for/with **(types of organizations/industries)** _____

_____

_____

_____

As an option, after you have used your positioning statement, you can add:
I am interested in learning more about the qualifications you are looking for and your performance expectations for the position.

The Interview

The Interview

Answering Commonly Asked Interview Questions

A major part of your interviewing strategy is being prepared to answer even the most challenging questions in a manner that demonstrates what you can do on the job. Keeping the strategic interviewing model in mind, use the information you have gathered in your research and your accomplishment stories to form the basis for answering most questions.

On the following pages are some of the more commonly asked interview questions (both traditional and behavior-based) and suggested strategies and techniques for providing good responses to some of them. They are grouped in five categories: Your Background Skills and Experience, Your Goals and Objectives, Your Education and Training, Your Weakness and Potential Problems, Sensitive Issues.

1. Your Background, Skills and Experience

When interviewers ask questions about your skills and experience, they are usually checking to see if they match their needs.

With broad general questions about your background, they also can check to see if you are displaying any negatives or large areas of irrelevant experience. Organizations are looking for people who can step right in and contribute to a group work situation. Interviewers, therefore, often start by verifying that your skills are both relevant and well developed.

o ·········· STRATEGY ·········· o

Questions in this category are sometimes called opportunity questions because they are an open invitation for well-prepared candidates to display their strengths. Questions of this type are predictable and you should be prepared to answer them. Minor variations of a basic formula work for all of them.

- **In your answer, use the competencies you have that are most relevant** to the position and organization, mention them by name and include an accomplishment story that illustrates more than one of them. This type of answer is considered behavior-based because it illustrates your skills with stories of how you actually behaved on the job. Your answers to these questions are generally behavior-based, whether the question is or not.

- **If you are especially well prepared, you can be even more focused** by offering several competencies, asking the interviewer which are the most relevant, and then providing an accomplishment story that illustrates one or more of the competencies the interviewer selected.

- **Your strategy in answering these questions is always to reassure your interviewer** that there is a match. Your confidence and tone are nearly as important as your words. Never volunteer negatives of any kind in response to these questions.

The Interview

 Questions About Your Background and Skills

TRADITIONAL:

- *Tell me about your last job.*

- *What aspects of your last work experience relate to this position?*

- *Why are you interested in working for this company?*

- *What contribution do you think you could make to this company?*

- *How would you describe your leadership style?*

BEHAVIOR-BASED:

- *Tell me about the parts of your background that qualify you for this position.*

- *What type of activities were you involved with in your last job that successfully used your management skills? Be specific.*

- *Give me examples of the types of experiences you have had managing people.*

- *In as much detail as possible, tell me the ways you used team building skills in your last job.*

SAMPLE Answers About Your Background and Skills

How would you describe your leadership style?

My leadership style has been described as firm and fair. In my job at Green Initiatives, I was asked to take over a department that had not been making its targets. It quickly became apparent that two of the team leaders were in constant conflict with each other over priorities. They could not get along. I talked to them individually and then together, reflecting back what each thought the priorities and problems were and re-emphasizing how I needed both of them to meet our targets. The result was, they started working together and started seeing me as their leader.

(Or, as with many questions, you can turn the questions around by asking:
What kind of leadership and management styles are predominant in this organization?)

Tell me about your last job.

As a Packaging Engineer, I led a team of three people that designed and implemented innovative packages for new products. Our task was to create packaging that was effective and had an expanded commercial shelf impact. I acted as the technical liaison with market research, advertising and manufacturing. One of our last products was designed and implemented in record time to meet a marketing deadline. We did in three months what typically had taken six. This enabled us to establish our product on the shelves before the competition.

What aspects of your last job relate to this position?

You mentioned that profitability was more of an issue than sales volume in two of your services. I faced a similar challenge in my last job. Our sales group was steadily increasing its sales volume, but profits were declining because they were selling the wrong service mix. I discovered that many of our salespeople simply did not understand some of the more complex services. They were selling the ones that were easier to sell, which were also low-profit services. I provided training and adjusted incentives, and profits went up 40% in one year.

Why are you interested in working for this company?

There are two reasons. First, you told me you have a need for someone to do expenditure planning, create new store cash flow models and provide profit and loss analysis. With a master's degree and five years of experience as a financial analyst doing budget forecasting and financial management in dynamic retail environments just like yours, I believe I would clearly be an asset to the company – especially when preparing those annual retail operating plans. Second, I've read your business plan and I'm impressed. I would like to be a part of a company that has grown from one small shop to 3,000 retail units in five years!

The Interview

2. Your Goals and Objectives

In exploring this category, the interviewer is exploring your interests, values or motivation and looking for candidates who value what the organization is doing and who are interested in the kind of work entailed in the open position.

The interviewer may also be concerned about the level and kind of motivation that propels you along your chosen career path and whether your career direction is consistent with the organization's direction and the thrust of the job. Your answers to questions on your goals and objectives provide important information on these topics.

○·············· **STRATEGY** ··············○

Your statements about your career goals need to be reasonably consistent with the open position and the way the organization normally operates.

- **You need to consider not only your own goals,** but what you know about the goals of the organization. For example, a statement that your long-term career goal is to be a VP of Sales may immediately end your candidacy for the opening of Assistant Director of Human Resources, or at least raise questions.

 # Questions About Your Goals and Objectives

TRADITIONAL:

- *What would your ideal career position be?*

- *Where would you like to be in three years? In five years?*

- *If you could begin your career over again, what would you do differently?*

BEHAVIOR-BASED:

- *What important career goals did you set and reach on your last job?*

- *Tell me about a time in your working history when you prioritized your career goals successfully.*

- *Career goals are often made to meet the expectations of a career management system. Tell me about a time when you took the initiative to set career goals and objectives, even though you were not directed by anyone to do so.*

The Interview

 # Answers About Your Goals and Objectives

What would your ideal career position be?

My ideal career position would be very similar to the position you are offering. Specifically, my ideal position would give me a chance to use my technical skills, leadership experience and product background to develop a new product line possibly in an international market. In my research about your company I discovered that your department is expanding the product line into European markets. I'd be interested in hearing more about that.

Where would you like to be in three years?

I would like to be working here three years from now. I have gathered enough information on your company to convince me this is the kind of organization I would be happy working for. I want to remain in financial services because I have always liked this line of work. I especially enjoy computers and would expect to learn some new software packages as well as using some of the software I already know. Three years from now I'd like to be using those skills to excel in your department.

Tell me about a time when you took the initiative to set career goals and objectives.

I'm the type of person who doesn't wait for an official policy to keep my career vital. One year ago, I sat down and developed a statement of career goals for myself, even though Amalgamated did not have a career management system. I used my career goal statement to talk to my boss about the coaching I would need from her to attain some of my more ambitious goals. The result of my effort was that I reached most of my career goals months before my target dates.

3. Your Education and Training

Questions about education and training are sometimes asked to determine if you have the knowledge it takes to do the job.

Some interviewers may also be attempting to determine your intellectual capacity, your interest in learning or whether your orientation is more practical or academic. Questions about your level of academic success may be an attempt to uncover your motivation.

For some positions, ongoing professional development is important, so the interviewer may ask about recent training courses.

STRATEGY

- **If you do not have the level of formal education normally associated with the job,** have an answer ready that demonstrates you have the skills and experience to do the job. Or, use an accomplishment story that describes how you held your own as a member of a more educated team.

- **If your education is above the expected level**, your strategy is to present yourself with humility and without intellectual superiority. Remember: Some interviewers may not have had the same educational opportunities you have.

- **You may wish to use an accomplishment story** about your education or training and the role it played in a relevant success. Another possibility is an accomplishment story about how you sought out a learning opportunity in order to succeed on a particular project.

 Questions About Your Education and Training

TRADITIONAL:

- *What formal education or training have you had?*

- *What part of that education or training prepares you to do this job*

- *What was the most important course you completed over the last year?*

BEHAVIOR-BASED:

- *Tell me about a time when you used your education and training.*

- *Pick a technical problem you had to solve, give the details in it, and tell me about what you did to create the solution to that problem.*

 Answers About Your Education and Training

Tell me what formal education or training you have had. Most people in this job start with an MBA.

Actually, I have an MS degree in International Business. I believe that particular program I attended is similar in terms of educational achievement to an MBA. My learning focused on business in the Pacific Rim area, and I believe this would be an asset to achieving the results you expect in this position. I think my experience is even more important, especially my experience in …

Tell me about a time when you used your education and training.

During my last project, it quickly became apparent that the team I had inherited needed a strong manager who could deal with the diverse backgrounds and experiences of the individuals on the team. In particular, there were three team members of widely different personal backgrounds who were sometimes in conflict and often simply ignored each other, even though they worked on the same projects. I had attended a training program called "Diversity and the Bottom Line" and used some of the techniques that I learned in that course. Specifically, I used a quick assessment to facilitate a discussion on how our differences influence our business relationships. It was well received. But more important, within a month, those three team members were regularly seeking each other's opinions and collaborating with each other.

The Interview

4. Your Weakness and Potential Problems

All candidates have weaknesses as well as strengths. The interviewer's job is to assess both. In addition to checking your qualifications, a good interviewer will always probe for weaknesses and potential problems.

There are two kinds of weaknesses an interviewer might be looking to uncover. The first is simply a lower level of experience or knowledge in some of the competencies the job requires. In this case, the interviewer must make an assessment on whether a candidate has the overall qualifications that best match the requirements of the job.

The second and more difficult kind includes personal weaknesses. Logically – and legally – the interviewer should be probing for only those that are job-related, such as the ability to effectively communicate with a diverse audience. But sometimes a candidate has a very serious personal problem that might impinge on job performance. Although it might be a personal problem, the interviewer who misses it could be seriously embarrassed later. Questions designed to bring serious issues to the surface are sometimes called knockout questions.

o············· **STRATEGY** ··············o

- **Your first strategy for dealing with questions that probe for weaknesses is to reassure the interviewer that you have no weaknesses** serious enough to rule you out of consideration. Then, you need to convince the interviewer that any job-related weaknesses you might have are easily overcome and outweighed by your strengths.

- **When answering the questions about weaknesses, keep in mind that none of us are perfect.** You need to recognize and understand your weaknesses. If you do not, when one of them is brought up in an interview, you will be unprepared and might make it appear worse than it is.

- **If you name weaknesses that are both relevant to the job at hand and significant,** you practically guarantee that you will be screened out.

- **The worst problem a candidate can create is to be appear to be deceitful.** There is a big difference between dishonesty and discretion – so make sure your answer is true and credible.

Questions About Your Weakness and Potential Problems

TRADITIONAL:

- *What are your strengths and weaknesses?*

- *Do you think that you might be overqualified for this position?*

- *What is the most serious criticism you have ever had from your boss?*

- *What would your previous boss say are your greatest strengths and weaknesses?*

- *What did your staff/peers think of you? How would they describe your work?*

- *Do you consider yourself to be a good leader/manager?*

- *How did you get along with other members of your team?*

BEHAVIOR-BASED:

- *Give me an example of a time when your biggest weakness at work kept you from reaching an important objective.*

- *Describe a time when you didn't work as hard as you could have.*

- *Give me an example of a time when you became bored with a project.*

- *Pick an example from your current job that would reflect on your ability to deal with pressure.*

- *This job will require you to work as part of a team of diverse backgrounds. Describe a time when you were not effective in managing a conflict at work.*

- *Individuals vary in their ability to use power to influence others. Give me a specific example of a time when you used power and it backfired.*

 ## Answers About Your Weakness and Potential Problems

WHAT ARE YOUR WEAKNESSES?

There are two classic answers to questions about weaknesses. The first is providing a weakness that is not really a weakness from the company's point of view.

Some people say that I am too rigid about accuracy and deadlines. And I must admit I am extremely fussy about both of them, but I have learned to discuss and set deadlines with my team that they find reasonable.

I have been criticized in the past for pressing too hard to close a sale. And I must admit I sometimes do press pretty hard. So I went for some additional training in relationship selling where I brushed up on my practical skills like probing, listening, handling objections and, of course, closing the sale.

The second answer is to redirect the focus of the question:

From what I know about this position so far, I can honestly say that I have no weaknesses that would prevent me from doing the job well. It looks exactly like the kind of job I want and I think I meet all of the qualifications. I have limited experience with X. However, in my previous job, I didn't know how to do Y. So I did some research and reading, and soon I was quite good at it.

The Interview

5. Sensitive Issues

Interviewers will sometimes include questions of a sensitive nature. Probing for potential weaknesses is one of the most difficult parts of interviewing and not all interviewers are skilled at it. Sometimes a less-skilled interviewer may ask inappropriate, even illegal, questions in an attempt to uncover potential weaknesses. A general guideline as to what is an appropriate (and legal) interview question is that it should be job-related.

The Equal Employment Opportunity Commission and Americans with Disabilities Act are intended to protect individuals. The hiring manager should be aware of relevant laws and not ask questions that violate them. However, not all hiring managers are up-to-date on these laws.

Inappropriate (and possibly illegal) questions include ones on the following topics:

- Birthplace
- Birthday
- Race
- Sexual orientation or preference
- Marital status; plans for having children
- Height and weight
- Hobbies or activities
- Disability or physical limitations

- Age
- Nationality
- Religion
- Arrest record
- Ages of children; child care plans
- History of drug or alcohol addiction
- Sentiments about unions

o ·········· **STRATEGY** ·········· o

- **Once a question is asked, you must determine how to respond.** Even if a question is sensitive (or even illegal), it requires a response of some sort. How you respond will say a lot about you as a person.

- **If you feel that a question is inappropriate,** try to determine what is behind the question by tactfully responding with questions such as:
  - Is there a concern about this area that relates to the position?
  - Can you help me understand how this relates to the job responsibilities?
  - I'm not sure how this question pertains to the job we are discussing. Can you elaborate?
  - While inappropriate questions can be frustrating, and even infuriating, you need to concentrate on advancing your career during the interview. If you wish to right an injustice, you are advised to do it at another time.

 Questions About Sensitive Issues

TRADITIONAL:

- *Why did you leave your previous employer?*

- *What did you dislike about your previous job?*

- *If I spoke to your present/previous manager, what would that person name as your greatest strengths and your greatest weaknesses?*

- *Are you opposed to drug testing?*

BEHAVIOR-BASED:

- *Tell me about a time when your work was criticized.*

- *Tell me about a time when you were not successful in coping with a pressure situation.*

- *Tell me about a time when you were not successful in adapting to change.*

- *Give me an example of an incident when you had a serious disagreement with your boss.*

 Answers About Sensitive Issues

WHY DID YOU LEAVE YOUR LAST EMPLOYER?

This is the most common example of a potentially sensitive question that is both legal and legitimate for a hiring manager to ask. You should expect to hear it and respond to it using your exit statement.

Tell me about a time when your work was criticized?

Two years ago I submitted a project plan to my boss. She called me into her office and criticized it from top to bottom. The conversation turned out to be one of the most productive we had ever had. It was a great learning experience for me because I had never done a project like that one before. As a result, I reworked the plan and the project went very well. My boss gave me a high performance rating that year mainly because of my success in managing that project.

The Interview

Handling the Salary Question in Your Interview

Your strategy needs to include a plan for handling questions about your current and anticipated salary. You want to delay discussion of compensation as long as possible; early discussions of compensation are always to your disadvantage. Revealing your most recent salary is likely to result in an offer that will be a bit (but not a lot) higher. If this is acceptable to you and you know your last salary was in line with industry standards, then reveal your most recent salary.

Go in with a Strategy

A basic strategy for dealing with salary questions consists of using three approaches:

- **Defer:** Don't reveal your salary requirements too early in the process.

- **Inquire:** Ask what the range is for the position you are discussing.

- **Reveal:** Give a range. This is where your research is critical.

This strategy is explained in further detail in the chart at the bottom of the following page.

Do Your Research Before the Interview

An essential part of your preparation before your interview is realizing what you're worth. Ideally, you can hold off the salary conversation until the negotiating stage, but that doesn't always work. You must be prepared to reveal.

It's important to research the marketplace to determine the salary range for someone with your background and experience. Establishing this "going rate" can be worth a lot of money to you.

Where to Look for Salary Ranges

Salary information is widely available on the Internet and elsewhere, but it varies dramatically in quality and accuracy. The business world is full of excellent – and very high-priced – salary surveys. These studies are conducted by consulting organizations on behalf of large corporations.

But don't be discouraged. There are all kinds of salary surveys and online salary calculators that are produced with consumers in mind at no-cost or low-cost options. Check out the Career Resource Network for the best of these.

When evaluating salary data, be sure that the data is current and determine whether it has been gathered by a reputable source. Ask yourself whether the salary data you're looking at comes from organizations that are comparable in size to the organizations you're targeting. Find out whether they represent the sector – public, private or not-for-profit – in which you are interested. Find out how many organizations have provided data for the survey – the more the better.

Consider whether the geography of the firms represented in the data matches your target market area. Also look closely at the job titles represented. In an age where titles are becoming more creative and less clear, it's important to compare required skills and scope of responsibility whenever possible.

Utilizing your information

Whether you have to use your research on your interview day or not, you will need it when it comes to the final negotiations. See later in this chapter for ways to negotiate your salary and your total compensation package.

Resources for Salary Ranges

- **The Internet:** You can easily find online salary calculators – some at low or no cost. Among the best websites are salary.com and salaryexpert.com.

- **Occupational Outlook Handbook:** Published by the U.S. Bureau of Labor Statistics, this is a nationally recognized source of career information. The book is designed to provide valuable assistance to individuals making decisions about their future work lives. Revised every two years, the handbook reveals earnings, describes what workers do on the job, the training needed and expected job prospects in a wide range of occupations. The U.S. Bureau of Labor Statistics also offers information at www.bls.gov.

- **Special issues of trade and professional journals:** Many of them do annual salary surveys. For example, the Chronicle of Higher Education does an annual almanac edition that would be invaluable for job seekers targeting academia.

- **Your professional or industry association:** Contact the particular association whose members have the kind of job you are targeting. Ask them if they publish a salary survey. If they don't, ask them who does.

Approaches/Answers to Salary Questions

APPROACH	STRATEGY/POSSIBLE ANSWERS
1. DEFER	**STRATEGY: Acknowledge question, but do not answer.** • Defer the conversation on grounds that more information is needed. If this does not work, go to step 2, inquire. *I couldn't really say without a complete understanding of what I would be accountable for. Can we talk more about … ?* *I think we may be in the same ballpark, but I need to know more about the job. Could you tell me a little more about …* *Salary is certainly an important consideration, but I need to know more about …* *My requirements are flexible.*
2. INQUIRE	**STRATEGY: Respond with a question, putting the ball back in their court.** • If this does not work, go to step 3, reveal. *What is the range you usually pay?* *Is that the mid-range or top range?* • Note: If their high end is your low end, react and keep the conversation going.
3. REVEAL	**STRATEGY: As a last alternative, give a range.** • Be sure you are happy with the low end of that range because you are signaling a willingness to accept it. *Based on what you have told me about this position, I think a range of ____ to ____ would be appropriate.*

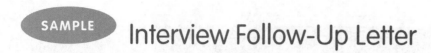

Interview Follow-Up Letter

Name
Address
City / State / Zip
Telephone Number • Email Address

Date

Ms. Anita Colton
Executive Vice President, Marketing
Lester International, Inc.
10023 Lester Boulevard
Cleveland, OH 51634

Dear Ms. Colton:

It was a pleasure to meet and talk with you yesterday. I appreciated the opportunity to learn more about Lester and the position of Vice President, North American Marketing.

One significant outcome of our meeting for me is that I am even more convinced that my previous experience with Johnson Corporation will prove extremely valuable in helping Lester meet their business goals in North America. I know the territory, and I certainly know your primary competitors in that territory very well.

Although we did not specifically talk about it, my experience in cultivating the Canadian market for Johnson is easily transferable to your stated goals of increasing your exposure and reputation in what has developed into a difficult marketplace for your products.

I am very interested in pursuing this position with you further and would welcome the opportunity to meet with you again, as well as any others in the company you feel would be appropriate. As you described the position, it appears to be the kind of challenge I excel at and have been hoping to find for some time.

Thank you for your time and interest. On the chance that you would like additional information or want to discuss next steps in more detail, I plan to call you early next week.

Sincerely,

Name

The Negotiating Process

Most people believe that salary is the only thing to be negotiated. In fact, nearly anything can be negotiated, including:

- **The job description** (or at least some of its details, including job title)
- **Starting date**
- **Vacations**
- **Decision-making authority**
- **Budget, resources and support**
- **Reporting relationships**

- **Relocation expenses**
- **Insurance and pension benefits**
- **Employment contracts**
- **Professional memberships** (and time to participate in them)
- **Stock options**
- **Bonus** (including a starting or sign-on bonus)

See more of what can be negotiated on page 167.

The extent to which you can negotiate successfully on all or some of the things mentioned depends on the nature and level of the job and the hiring policies of the company. In general, the higher your position and the smaller the company, the more you can negotiate; for a lower position in a larger company, your negotiating room may be more limited. Remember that any negotiating should begin only after an offer has been extended.

Guidelines for Negotiating

- **Do not be afraid to negotiate.** Most organizations will not withdraw an offer just because you make a reasonable request. Companies do get a sense of what you will be like as an employee by the behavior you display during negotiations, so exercise discretion.
- **Do not reveal your salary requirements too early in the process** or you may lose your future leverage.
- **Do not exaggerate your present income.** It is easy for an organization to verify any figure that you give them; some even ask for a W-2 or tax return.
- **Resist accepting an offer on the spot, no matter how good it seems.** Always ask for time to think it over. This strategy might provide you with an opportunity to negotiate a better package. A quick acceptance could also be taken as a sign they offered too much.
- **If you cannot get the salary offer increased,** you might try for a guaranteed bonus, a performance incentive or added benefits.
- **Negotiate cash compensation first,** then consider the other benefits and perks to complete the total compensation package.
- **Include in your thinking all cash compensation, bonuses, profit sharing and tangible non-cash compensation** (such as a company car or club membership), as well as benefits (such as medical).
- **If you do not meet with any success in your negotiations concerning the present,** concentrate on the future such as a review in six months, an automatic increase after 12 months or a performance incentive.
- **When negotiating, be enthusiastic about everything:** the job, the future boss and the opportunity. Stay entirely positive.
- **Obtaining top dollar for one's services is not an easy matter and requires some finely honed negotiating skills.** Keep your discussions of money on an impersonal level and be as businesslike and logical. Try to do it in more than one conversation so you can get objective advice between discussions.
- **As crucial as salary is, there are other important considerations.** These include scope of responsibility and degree of autonomy, as well as non-cash compensation. Do not ignore or underrate them.

Negotiating Salary

Before you begin the negotiation process, research the marketplace and determine the salary range for someone with your background and experience. The Internet is a good source for this type of research (see pages 156-157 for more on that).

Discreetly talking to people inside of the company, if possible, enables you to get information about compensation practices and to uncover the internal salary range for the job you want.

The second thing you need to do before entering into negotiations is to be clear about what salary range you need and will accept.

Most large corporations have structured compensation programs with established salary ranges for most positions. Even when a company claims that a salary is open, you can be sure that the people responsible for filling the particular position are conducting their search within the constraints of a specific salary range. In addition, companies with ranges are seeking to bring people in at or below the midpoint of the range.

Exceptions to this general rule exist for smaller or less-structured firms for salaries of top executives (i.e., CEO, CFO, COO) and for newly created positions. Obviously these situations present your widest latitude for negotiating.

Two Negotiating Scenarios

Making a counteroffer – It is usually to your advantage to have the employer make the first mention of numbers to establish the floor amount. The next move is your counteroffer.

Scenario #1

Suppose you learned that the approximate range for a certain job is $75,000 to $90,000 and the employer makes you an offer of $81,000. You were making $80,000 at your last job and believe your background and experience now make you worth $85,000. Your counteroffer may sound something like this:

> *I really want to work for you because the position is an excellent one, and I know I can produce results for you. Given my experience and track record, I feel I am worth $89,000.*

This leaves room for the employer to raise the initial offer and for you to come down somewhat in the hopes that the final offer will be the $85,000 you want.

When you make a counteroffer, be flexible and keep the negotiation open at all times. Do not be afraid of silence. If the response is a firm no, you will need to move your negotiations to a non-cash option. However, your natural desire to get the job should not prevent you from selling your background and experience a little more.

Scenario #2

The employer suggests a salary of $90,000 and you have been earning a bit more than that. Your counteroffer may sound something like:

> *If we agree to $90,000, would it be possible to include three weeks vacation rather than two? Or: If I agree to that figure, would it be possible to review my salary after three months? I believe you will be well satisfied with the contributions I make.*

Remember that while a counteroffer from you may be expected as part of the negotiation process, the employer will also expect that you have left room to negotiate downward a bit. The employer might increase the initial offer somewhat, but will expect you to lower your counteroffer.

Before making the counteroffer, preface your remarks by expressing a genuine interest in the position and explaining that, based on your experience, skills and track record, you feel you are worth more.

Negotiating the Total Compensation Package

Listed below are suggested non-cash compensation items you should consider when negotiating your final compensation package. After the obvious financial benefits (commission, bonus, stock, profit sharing, pension, 401K), there are numerous non-cash possibilities that can provide significant financial advantages for you.
Do not attempt to run through this entire list with a prospective employer. Read the benefit brochures and other company materials first. Then ask questions to get the information you need on the different programs. Afterwards, prioritize and concentrate on negotiating those that are most important to you.

MEDICAL PLAN
- Dental plan
- Eye care
- Counseling
- Company share
- Deductible
- Percentage reimbursed
- Choice of care providers

INSURANCE:
LIFE, DISABILITY, ACCIDENT
- Size and scope of benefits
- Cost to employee
- Payments
- Company share/your payments
- Travel insurance in addition to life insurance and accidental death
- Insurance protection for personal liability arising from execution of job duties

COMPANY-PAID
RELOCATION ASSISTANCE
- Moving costs
- Hotel and travel costs for employee and family
- Mortgage assistance and brokerage fees
- Installation of carpets, appliances

VACATION
- Number of days first year
- Schedule for subsequent years
- Compensation for unused days
- Supplemental vacation

PAID HOLIDAYS
- Number per year
- Flexibility of usage
- Personal holidays
- Compensation for unused days
- Carryover or accrual provisions

AUTOMOBILE/
AUTOMOBILE EXPENSES
- Company car (make/model, frequency of turnover, personal use, charge for personal use, shared by others, gas and upkeep)
- Car allowance in lieu of company car (flat or mileage basis; tax implications and offsets)

EXPENSE ACCOUNTS
- Floating allowance basis
- Reimbursement basis
- Commuting costs
- Company-provided or paid parking

COMPANY PRODUCT
DISCOUNT PROGRAMS
- University tuition grant for dependent children
- Other non-company consumer product or "plus" programs

CAFETERIA OR DINING ROOM
- Meals fully paid or supported
- Value in pre-tax dollars

AIR TRAVEL
- First class
- Company-paid airline, VIP lounge

CLUB MEMBERSHIPS OR DUES
- Health/golf/tennis clubs
- Luncheon clubs
- Facilities available to families

PROFESSIONAL/TRADE
ASSOCIATION MEMBERSHIPS
OR DUES
- Certification or license costs reimbursed
- Costs of participation in association meetings or programs

IN-TOWN COMPANY
COURTESY APARTMENTS
- Availability
- Use by employee only or family

EDUCATIONAL
ASSISTANCE PROGRAMS
- Percentage of actual costs reimbursed
- Ceiling
- Work-related only or other limitations

EMPLOYEE
ASSISTANCE PROGRAMS
- Counseling for employee or family (substance abuse, financial problems)

COMPANY-PAID PROFESSIONAL
ASSISTANCE PROGRAMS
- Income tax filing
- Financial investment planning
- Legal services

ANNUAL PHYSICAL EXAMINATION
- Employee/family members

Closing the Deal

Now that you are close to having made your job campaign a successful one, it is very important that you not do anything that might compromise your chances. This is not the time to take foolish risks or to stop doing your homework. Too many sure things have been known to slip away at the last minute simply because they were taken for granted.

Here are some ways to protect yourself:

- Agree on a decision date and be sure to give your answer by that date.

- Do not completely stop your search project or cut off other options until you have actually started work. Until you are on the payroll, you have nothing more than the employer's word.

- If possible, try to get the offer in writing. A letter confirming employment and the terms is the most common form. If you are currently employed, it would be unwise to resign before getting written confirmation.

- If you do not get the offer in writing, you can write a letter to them confirming the terms of agreement.

- Be certain no contingencies remain up in the air. For example, have all reference and security checks been made? If required, have you passed the medical exam?

- Do not spread the word about your new employment until you are truly on board. Keep the offer to your family and close associates until it is finalized.

- Once you have started your new job, remember to close out your search properly and prepare for managing your new career. This is covered in the chapter for Milestone 10.

Tips and Techniques

Handling Multiple Offers

It is not entirely unlikely that you will find yourself in the position of receiving two or more offers at the same time. Here are suggested strategies:

- **Buy as much time as you can.** Do not be afraid to ask for the time you need to make the best decision and to consider – or cultivate – other offers. A company is unlikely to withdraw an offer because you ask for a bit more time to consider it. You might say something like: *I'm very excited about this opportunity and your offer. Yours is very much the kind of company I have been looking for. Naturally, I want to discuss it with my family. May I get back to you on Monday?*

  Or, you could extend the process by asking to see the benefit package in detail.

- **Talk with the other companies.** Use the time to get in touch with other companies you have had discussions with and try to accelerate their process. You may want to tell them about the other offer, although mentioning the organization's name is usually not a good idea.

- **You might say something like:** *I wanted to get to you right away because I've received an offer from another organization. I continue to be very interested in your company, and you have expressed some interest in me. I wonder if there is anything we can do to accelerate the process?*

- **There are many reasons why companies take a long time making hiring decisions.** If you are a strong candidate, the idea of losing you might jolt them into action. If you are likely to accept the other offer, you have very little to lose.

Letter of Offer of Employment

I am pleased to confirm our offer of employment to join International Industries, Inc. as Vice President of Marketing. Accepting this offer means you will be responsible for our new Pacific Rim territory, performing the duties specified in the enclosed job description. This letter summarizes the details of this offer and your employment relationship with us.

This offer of employment includes:
- a beginning salary of $110,000 a year with a six-month review in the first year.
- three weeks of vacation the first year; four weeks after the first year; sabbatical after five years.
- company-paid relocation from Minnesota to Japan.
- profit sharing, 401K and benefit plan as outlined in the attached benefits package.

This offer is contingent upon:
- satisfactory employment verification and reference checks.
- satisfactory verification of your identity and right-to-work in the U.S. under the 1986 Immigration Reform and Control Act (completion of INS Form I-9).
- execution of a Confidentiality and Invention Agreement.
- completion of our enrollment package.

Please sign below to indicate your acceptance of this offer, which is good until (date). I look forward to your accepting this offer and joining our team. If you have any questions, please do not hesitate to call me.

Sincerely,

I have read this letter and accept the terms and conditions of employment.

_____   _____
Signature   Date

Enclosures

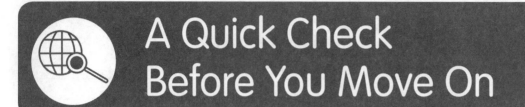

A Quick Check
Before You Move On

Now you're getting down to it! You're in the crucial stage of your search. There's much to gain, and much to potentially lose, so you want to handle these discussions with great care. CRN can help.

Before you leave this milestone:

Go to Career Resource Network (CRN) to find:

- Tips and e-learning on how to handle questions you are asked and how to formulate questions you'll want to ask during interviews

- Ways to sharpen up your accomplishment stories, which you'll use on interviews. Think SOAR (Situation, Obstacles, Action, Results)

- Descriptions of the various types of interviews, including the telephone interview and the second interview, and how to manage them

- Tips on the negotiating process, including what to negotiate and when. Access to salary calculators, local market and relocation information

- Samples of letters and email messages you can use to follow up on interviews, or to accept or reject a job offer

On interviews and in the negotiating process, it's important that you have your message "down." You want to be able to call up and articulate the right material on a moment's notice, so take some time to rehearse (possibly with the aid of another) before you go live.

Milestone 10

Transition into a New Position

Why this Milestone is Important...

Congratulations! You have managed your search project well and have landed! You are excited and eager to move on with your career, and rightfully so. But we have added this last milestone for a very good reason: Your job search project may have ended, but your career is just beginning a new chapter.

Maintain Your Network

If your search was of average length or more, you probably got your message out to a lot of people, and many of them may have talked to their contacts about you. An important component in closing out your search is notifying your contacts of your success and new status and, just as important, thanking them for their support during your transition.

You worked hard building and maintaining your network of contacts. It is too valuable to lose. Decide who you want to keep in your network long term. Develop a communications strategy so that you regularly stay in contact with them.

Although it might be easier, do not just send a 'batch' message to let everyone know you're hired. Call or send individual emails to people who helped in your job search process. After that, perhaps you may want to send the 'batch' message to Facebook friends.

Also make sure you update your online profiles, especially LinkedIn.

You Need to Prepare for Your Transition

There are a few things you can do to get off on the right foot in your new job:

- **Get involved in your announcement.** Ask to be involved in your announcement so that you can maximize as much as possible how you are seen, presented and positioned.

- **Define responsibilities, expectations and issues.** Develop a list of your own questions and a list of topics to discuss with your new boss so that responsibilities, roles and expectations are clear and well-defined. Identify the issues you feel are facing you in your new position: the problems, commitments and pending decisions. Think about and weigh the favorable and unfavorable conditions of your new job.

- **Develop an entry strategy.** Develop a strategy for how you will get more of the critical information you need about the organization, the people, the work and the norms so that you build solid relationships with your new boss, peers and staff members.

Questions to Explore

- *If I have been considering another offer, have I informed the competing organization of my decision?*

- *Have I closed the loop in organizations where I have networked extensively so that I can preserve good relationships?*

- *Have I informed all recruiters with whom I have been working?*

- *Have I called or written to thank the contacts who provided me with information and support during my search project?*

- *Have I organized my database and put a plan in place to maintain the network I have built?*

- *Have I developed a plan for entry into my new organization?*

Suggested Actions

- **Tie up all the loose ends from your job search:**
    - Contact other organizations you have been negotiating with.
    - Thank your contacts for their help and let them know how they can reach you in the future.
    - Organize a database of your contacts so you can stay in touch.
    - Keep in touch with your contacts on a regular basis.
- **Clarify expectations of your new role,** identify immediate challenges and be sure you clearly understand the internal situation of which you are now a part.
- **Get involved in how your new position is announced to the various stakeholders.** This first announcement is generally very short, but because it makes a lasting impression, it is worth thinking through.
- **Establish plans for building solid relationships** and clarifying expectations with your new boss, peers and staff members.
- **Create a strategy for analyzing the readiness of the organization and your subordinates** to accept any changes you plan to initiate.
- **Start working on your professional development early in your new position.** Use your search experience to increase your new effectiveness on the job, build new skills and enhance your overall marketability. Consider enlisting a professional executive coach to assist you.

Closing Out Your Search

Closing out your job search means ending any other negotiations that may be pending with other companies and contacting any recruiters you may have been working with to let them know where you can be found in the future. It also means communicating with your network of contacts to thank them for their help and to express an interest in staying in touch with them.

Contact Other Companies

Contact any other companies you have been negotiating with – or networking extensively with – and tell them of your decision. You can do this by telephone for expediency, but you will also want to follow-up with a more detailed letter or email. Keep in mind when writing your letter that you will want to leave the door open to any potential opportunities in the future. If you already have a new business card, include it with your letter.

Notify Your Contacts

After all your work, you certainly do not want to cut yourself off from the contacts you worked so hard to develop. They can be just as valuable to you in the future as sources of information, professional alliances and, of course, networking contacts should you find yourself in search again.

- Write, email or call each of your contacts – including recruiters that have been especially helpful – to advise them of your new status. Let them know how they can contact you in the future and thank them for their support, information and referrals (if appropriate) during your search project.

- Review your list of contacts and decide which ones you would like to be part of your active network in the future. Set up a database to help you keep track of your continuing contact with them. In your correspondence with these contacts, suggest ways that you can continue to be helpful to each other.

Consistent and persistent utilization of your network can reap long-term career benefits for you and is simply part of good career management. Look for opportunities to celebrate other people's successes with a note or call, regularly keep in touch by passing along information or articles you come across and, of course, be a source of support and information to them should they (or any of their contacts) find themselves in job search.

Preparing Your Announcement

An announcement can range from a formal press release to the public to an internal notice to different parts of the organization.

Whatever form it takes, it typically sets the tone for how you are formally and publicly introduced into a new organization and can leave a lasting first impression on people. It is well worth your time to determine in advance how you can influence your announcement – or perhaps even write it.

In any new job, it is important to think about the impact your appointment might have on an organization and your acceptance into it.

Consider these questions:

- *What is the change? Why is it being made?*

- *Where is the person who had the job before me going? (optional)*

- *Why was I selected?*

- *What are my intentions, plans or goals?*

- *Is there any controversy surrounding me or my new position? Why?*

- *What information about my background do I want people to know?*

- *What particular things about me do I not want mentioned?*

- *What is the political climate and how does it relate to me?*

Assimilating Into Your New Position

The company impressed you. You wanted to work there, and you got the job. Now, you need to think about how you can best assimilate into the organization. Lee Hecht Harrison's Executive Assimilation Coaching provides the necessary strategy and structure to help new or recently promoted executives assess their personal development as it relates to an organization's culture and expectations, and assists in developing measurable outcomes within the critical first six months.

The following information is adapted from the initial steps of the Executive Assimilation Coaching approach. It will enable you to put together a strategy and action plan to facilitate your own successful assimilation. Even without your own professional coach to guide you, you can use some of the same principles used by Lee Hecht Harrison coaches. As you get started in your new position, pay attention to these four areas, which are discussed in detail on the following pages:

1. Reading the Culture

One of the first goals in successful assimilation into a new company or new work group is to identify the cultural norms and styles of the organization, your manager, peers and direct reports. This is a critical step in understanding the similarities and avoiding potential mismatches between your style and the company's culture.

You probably gained an impression of the culture during your research and interview activities. Now is the time to refine what you know. The organizational culture sometimes can be summed up in one sentence:

THIS IS THE WAY WE DO THINGS AROUND HERE.

Norms are part of the culture of any organization. And they are not usually written down anywhere. They are ways of behaving at work, a set of behaviors that have evolved over time. You chose this organization because it fit your ideas of what you wanted. Now, as a new person, you need all the information you can gather about an organization's culture. If this information were recorded as a list of beliefs, values, or even do's and don'ts, what would they be?

They are norms about how people behave in a work group and how work gets done. These group norms are not always obvious and are difficult to explain to someone outside the group. They are virtually never verbalized.

2. Building Alliances and Influencing Others

The appointment of a new employee almost always creates change in the organization's structure and social fabric. You need to establish meaningful and genuine connections with peers, senior executives, customers and employees, to build trust and credibility quickly. These connections provide the foundation for you to contribute effectively to the organization. Moving too quickly to what you can deliver without building a positive alliance can alienate others and undermine essential cooperation and support.

- *What are others responsible for? What is important to them? What do they need?*

- *What works for them? What doesn't?*

- *How does my job fit with what they do? How can I make their jobs easier?*

- *How does my work fit into the general scheme of things?*

- *Who are the people in control of the resources that make my work happen?*

- *How can I collaborate with them? What can I offer them?*

Look for ways to support the needs of others. Sometimes moves like this made early on can have lasting effects. Make as many contacts with peers as possible in the beginning while it is still acceptable to ask questions. Meet as many people individually as you can and as quickly as possible.

Build Relationships. Naturally, you will need to build working relationships with your subordinates quickly. Think carefully about what impression you want to convey and then find the means to do it. You will probably use a combination of group and individual meetings. It may be better to begin with individual meetings to gather information before staging a group meeting.

You may want to ask individuals such questions as:

- *What are your current activities?*

- *What is your professional background?*

- *Briefly describe yourself. What would you like me to know about you?*

- *What do you see as the strengths and weaknesses of the organization? Of our work group?*

- *What are your ideas about things we should stop doing? Things we should start doing?*

- *Are there any promises or commitments made to you I should know about?*

- *What do you want to know about me? Is there anything specific that you need from me?*

3. Determining and Aligning Expectations

Understanding what business results are expected, by whom, and in what priority is the next phase of successful assimilation. Key to this step is establishing agreement on what success will look like and how it will be measured. Naturally this begins with your boss, and probably will not be entirely defined in just one conversation.

Following are some things you want to know.

Even if you asked some of these questions as part of the interviewing process, asking them on the job is a way to fine-tune the answers.

- *What am I responsible for?*
- *What are the expectations for me immediately and over the long run?*
- *What are my boss' priorities? What is important?*
- *What kind of working relationship does my boss prefer?*

You may also want to ask questions like:

- *What was the person I am replacing like?*
- *What did that person accomplish?*
- *Did that person have any difficulties?*
- *What is currently going on in the organization that I need to know?*
- *What pending promises, commitments or key decisions will affect me?*
- *Which key people should I meet?*
- *What procedural, informational and meeting expectations apply to me?*

4. Focusing on Early Impact Projects

It is with the best intentions that most new executives try to make a broad and significant impact. However, the long-term focus should be balanced with the short-term, since you need to demonstrate your effectiveness early on in order to become established as a force in the organization. If you try to spend time on every possible project or initiative, your efforts will be significantly diluted.

Ask yourself:

- *Considering all that I have learned so far, what projects are the most important to undertake in my first year?*
- *Which projects are long-term and which short-term?*
- *Of the short-term projects, which are most likely to create an early positive impact on the organization?*

Maintaining Your Career Momentum

Landing a great new job does not mean you can sit back and let your career evolve. There are a few things you need to do to maintain your career momentum. Some of them you learned during your search project.

Continue to Survey Your Professional Environment

Just as you did early in your search project, continue to survey your professional environment regularly, keeping current on what is happening in your industry and profession.

Industries and professions change and you need to know how the changes will affect your future employability.

- *How will your profession fit into the future plans of your new employer?*

- *How will it fit in the long term in other organizations you might want to pursue in the future?*

- *What do you need to do to enhance your skills and competencies in the short and long term so you can remain at the top of your game?*

- *Should you consider working with a professional coach to help you do that?*

Occasionally Redefine Your Professional Objective

Whether you consider this new job the best possible next career move or a transitional one, you need to continue to redefine where you want your career to go next. Maybe you have your eye on your new boss's job; perhaps your ultimate dream is to head a particular department, unit or company – maybe even your own company.

Assess your mission, skills, interests, values and traits from time to time to determine whether any of them have changed. Just as your professional objective set the tone for your search project, it also sets the tone for managing your career.

Always Have a Communications Strategy

Knowing the importance of accomplishment stories in job search – and remembering how difficult it can sometimes be to recall and develop them – resolve to document your new accomplishment stories on an ongoing basis in your new job. Keep a log or journal of accomplishments, successes, goals met, initiatives taken, problems solved and other positive events. Get in the habit of taking inventory of this valuable information and writing it down on a weekly basis.

And, always, always, keep your resume up-to-date. You never know when another opportunity might present itself.

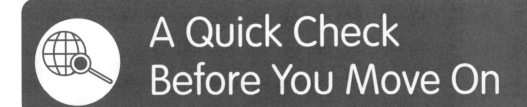

A Quick Check Before You Move On

Congratulations to you! You deserve congratulations because you've worked hard on your search, and you've also worked hard to develop and expand your network. So don't abandon it now! Take a look at these suggestions.

Before you leave this milestone:

Go to Career Resource Network (CRN) to find:

- Tips on how to handle the completion of your search process while keeping your network relationships up and running

- Samples of letters and email messages you can use to let people know of your success

- Ways to contribute to the announcement of your arrival

- Suggestions on how to maintain your career momentum, and considerations for assimilating quickly and effectively into your new position

What you do in the first three months on your new job may be critical to your long-term success, so it's important that you do well quickly. People joining a new organization face special challenges, including lack of familiarity with the culture and the unwritten rules, and often an organizational prejudice against outsiders. Be realistic in anticipating some skepticism about you and your arrival, and work hard to score some early successes while you uncover the way things truly work in the new organization. CRN suggests a few books you may find helpful in transitioning to your new job.

Ongoing Use of CRN

When you complete your program with Lee Hecht Harrison, you will be provided free, unlimited access to the Career Resource Network Alumni site - with the exception of the premium databases such as SkillSoft. Much of what you'll find there is exactly what you had during your LHH career transition program, including:

- E-learning, podcasts, and interactive tools and documents

- Sample resumes, cover letters, email messages and other documents

- All your personal saved documents and links from CRN

- Access to an LHH company-wide networking database

- Unlimited use of LHH's proprietary resume services

As your career moves forward, we want you to remain connected with Lee Hecht Harrison.
Best of luck to you in your new position!

Glossary of Terms

Accomplishment Statements:
Brief statements that capture the actions you took and the results you achieved. You put these in the content of your resume.

AIM:
Lee Hecht Harrison's proprietary three-stage business approach to career transition. The acronym stands for Assess Opportunity, Implement Search and Manage Transition.

Career Vision:
Where you want to be in your work life in five years. Exactly what you would like your work situation to be. When you look at your life as a whole, what part you want your career to play.

Chronological Resume:
Lists work experience in reverse chronological order, outlining your job history from the most recent job backwards, with greater emphasis on the most recent job. This is the most frequently used – and accepted format.

CRN:
The Career Resource Network is Lee Hecht Harrison's proprietary website designed to assist you in virtually all areas of your search. The website address is Career.lhh.com. Once you register for the CRN, you are a member for life.

Direct Mail:
Involves sending letters or emails to people who have never heard of you and who have no connection with you at all. The success rate of getting to a hiring manager through this means is low.

Ecopreneurship:
Launching a business with a green focus. Most ecopreneurs create a niche market in fields that have given them the market advantage while also providing positive results for the environment.

Entrepreneurship:
Being your own boss or owning your own business. Basically, there are four entrepreneurial options: becoming a consultant, acquiring a franchise, buying a business or starting a business. The decision of being self-employed is based primarily on personal factors.

Executive Search Firms:
Also commonly known as recruiters or headhunters, they work on the behalf of employers, not job seekers. They frequently recruit people who are employed, as well as active job seekers. Beware of any firm that asks you for a fee.

Exit Statement:
Answers the question: Why are you looking for a new job? An effective exit statement is brief, non-defensive and positive.

Functional Resume:
Designed to stress the qualifications of the job seeker, with less emphasis on specific employers and dates. This is particularly suitable for job seekers who want to make a significant change in their field or functional areas.

LinkedIn:
Career-related site that can be used as an effective networking tool. It is the most professional of all social media sites and a must for job seekers. Make sure you set up your social media profile here.

Personal Marketing Plan:
Helps you organize and prioritize your job search and keeps your productivity high. It includes your professional objective, positioning statement, target market and target list.

Positioning Statement:
A fundamental communications tool that will be used throughout your search. Basically, it answers who you are. In a few sentences, it tells your profession, expertise, types of organizations in which you have worked and your unique strengths.

Glossary of Terms

Professional Objective:
This defines the kind of work you want to do within your profession, making it easier for people you talk with to know exactly what it is you are looking for and be of optimal assistance.

Resume:
A key sales tool that represents an overview of what you have done in the past and implies what you can do for a potential employer in the future

SELL:
Lee Hecht Harrison's recommended approach when meeting with hiring managers. The acronymn stands for Summarize your message, Explore their needs, Link your benefits, Leverage a next contact.

Skills:
These are acquired through education and experiences of all kinds (such as employment, volunteer work and life experience) and represent your principal assets in your job market.

SIC, NAICS codes:
In conducting industry research, Standard Industrial Classification (SIC) codes or North American Industry Classification System (NAICS) codes can be useful.

Six Degrees of Separation:
Long-standing theory of networking that says you can reach anyone on the planet through six steps. Your friends and close acquaintances are at the first degree. In job search, you usually succeed at the second or third degree of separation.

SMART:
Lee Hecht Harrison's recommended approach when meeting with your general networking contacts. The acronymn stands for Summarize your message, Marketing plan, Ask questions, Referrals, Trade Information.

SOAR:
A technique used to develop your accomplishments into stories that showcase your skills. In an interview, your SOAR answer provides specific information on the Situation, Obstacles, Action and Results.

Summary Statement:
Usually the first thing on your resume. Its purpose is to encapsulate the experience, areas of expertise and professional skills detailed in the body of your resume. This may be very similar to your positioning statement.

Target Market:
Describes where you want to work. It defines the types of organizations in which you want to invest the most search time. Job seekers determine their Target Market by evaluating clear criteria for the group of organizations they plan to pursue including: geographic boundaries, industries, size of companies and preferred organizational culture.

The Four C's:
This is part of the strategic interviewing process. You are looking for four things in an interview: Competence, Compatibility, Chemistry and Compensation. The interviewer is looking for all of the same things except for compensation.

The Ladder:
A concept that relates networking to climbing a ladder. You start at the bottom with your Inner Circle – friends, relatives and close acquaintances. Then you work your way up to the top (Level One) and the hiring manager.

Total Compensation Package:
When negotiating the final terms of your employment, you should consider many things beyond just salary, such as medical plan, insurance, vacations, educational assistance, 401K and much more.

Directory

Directory

Your Notes

Your Notes

Your Notes